The night is dark and silent –
but you're not alone.

Silent
Night

TEN TALES OF THE SUPERNATURAL BY...

JOAN AIKEN

TERENCE BLACKER

HELEN DUNMORE

SUSAN GATES

LESLEY HOWARTH

TONY MITTON

K.M.PEYTON

CELIA REES

JAMES SWALLOW

PATRICK WOOD

Silent Night

Scholastic Children's Books,
Commonwealth House, 1-19 New Oxford Street,
London, WC1A 1NU, UK
a division of Scholastic Ltd
London ~ New York ~ Toronto ~ Sydney ~ Auckland
Mexico City ~ New Delhi ~ Hong Kong

First published by Scholastic Ltd, 2002

ISBN 0 439 98242 1

Printed and bound by Cox and Wyman Ltd, Reading, Berks.

10 9 8 7 6 5 4 3 2 1

Contents

Longship
Patrick Wood   1

The Knock at the Door
Helen Dunmore   22

No Man's Land
Susan Gates   39

Lady in Blue, Unidentified
Terence Blacker   58

Mummy! Mummy!
K.M. Peyton   80

Babushka
Tony Mitton   107

The Ghost of Christmas Shopping
Lesley Howarth   114

Wee Robin
Joan Aiken   134

Snowblind
James Swallow   143

The Devil's Dozen
Celia Rees   162

Longship

Patrick Wood

Afterwards, Mackey wouldn't even talk about it unless he got blind drunk. "Muster been that fish that gorrim," he'd say then, the beer slopping in his glass as his hand trembled. "Bloody great pre'storic thing. Muster chewed 'im to rags an' swallered 'im down." Sometimes he described the screams, or the clouds of blood in the churning water.

I wished I could believe Mackey's lurid explanation. But in fact there had been no screams, or blood. Mackey had been face down on the deck when Larsen went overboard. He hadn't seen it happen. I had, and I wasn't going to tell a soul, no matter how drunk I was.

It had still been dark when I got to the quayside that cold December morning. The storm had blown

1

over and the sky prickled with stars. I strained my eyes to the east for the first grey smudge of dawn but there was no sign of it.

Out on the water, red and green navigation lights marked channels through the harbour. The dim shapes of boats at anchor rose and dipped with the swell. A skein of coloured bulbs hung swaying from a pair of lampposts near to me. In the choppy black water their reflection looked like a submerged necklace of precious stones, writhing gently in the running tide.

Larsen was already aboard the *Shelty*. I could hear him banging about in the wheelhouse, making ready to put out to sea. There were no other sounds except the clop of waves against the harbour walls and the clank of wire rigging against the aluminium masts of the boats in the yacht club dock. It was too early even for the gulls.

I lingered on the quay, enjoying the crisp feel of newly fallen snow beneath my boots. The air was cold enough to scrape the back of my throat with each breath I drew, and I was sure there would be another blizzard before the end of the week.

A car door slammed somewhere behind me and in a few seconds Mackey was at my side, already fumbling with the lid of his Thermos.

"A'reet, Russ? What yer ganna miss this mornin'?"

2

"Double 'ist'ry."

Mackey shrugged and thrust a plastic cup of steaming tea into my hands. "But yer'd rather earn a bit o' money for some Christmas presents, eh? Gettin' summat nice for yer gran?"

"Bottle o' Bell's and a Barbara Cartland. An' ah'm mackin' a fish mobile out of tinfoil for Mr Scratch."

"Oh aye? That's canny." With a quick movement, Mackey dashed a slug from his hip flask into his own cup of tea. "Medicinal purposes," he explained.

The *Shelty*'s engine clattered into life. A cloud of oily smoke drifted along the quay.

"What you missing this morning?" Larsen demanded as I jumped down beside him on the *Shelty*'s deck.

"Double 'ist'ry. But we break up for Christmas day after tomorrer. No one's ganna care."

When Mackey joined us Larsen swayed towards him and sniffed. "You been drinking already, Mack?"

"Drinkin'?" Mackey looked astonished. "It's me antiseptic, man." He pointed at his face. "Doctor's orders. Moush ulther."

Larsen grunted. "Well, just watch your footing, that's all. Coming in after you to haul you out wouldn't be my idea of fun at this time of year."

3

We cast off the *Shelty*'s moorings and the trawler nosed its way towards the harbour bar, Larsen at the wheel.

"What's 'e tarkin' aboot?" muttered Mackey. "Ah could 'op round this boat blinefurled!" But I knew this was just bravado. Mackey would never say such a thing to the captain's face. He feared the big man's temper and his strength.

After glancing over his shoulder to make sure he hadn't been heard, Mackey leaned closer towards me. "Look a' this!" he said. He reached into his oilskin coat and drew a red and green tinsel star halfway out of his pocket. "'Bout time this tub had a bit o' seasonal decoration." He slapped the *Shelty*'s gunwale, then nodded back towards the wheelhouse. "An' it might just cheer the ahld bugger up an' ahll. What d'yer reckon?"

Looking aft, I could just make out Larsen's face in the light from the *Shelty*'s instrument panel. His thick brows were knotted into a frown as he stared out into the darkness, and his big fists gripped the spokes of the wheel so tightly that the knuckles shone.

"If ah were you," I said, "ah'd wait for the right moment before yer ask 'im."

We rounded the pier and the wind bit into us. I crouched down to try and escape the worst of it, my back against a coil of rope, hugging myself to

4

keep warm. The cuffs of my rough sweater chafed the backs of my hands.

Dawn was at last beginning to break. As we passed St Ninian's Point I could just make out the ruins of the priory against the greying sky.

Larsen leaned out of the wheelhouse, his beard blowing. "We're headed for Winchey Sands," he shouted. "Take us about half an hour. Teach the lad some history till we get there, Mack."

Larsen didn't really care if I missed school to come fishing. He was different from the other fishermen, always doing things his own way: leaving earlier, coming back later, avoiding the usual fishing grounds to cast his nets in untried waters. Probably why he couldn't afford to be fussy about his crew.

None of the other skippers I'd asked would take me out on a weekday. They talked about how I should think of my future and finish my schooling first. But they didn't really mean it. Round here there isn't any future, at least not the kind where it makes much difference whether you finished school or not.

Since they've closed the pits and run the shipyards down there's nothing to do up here but fish. Even that's not the living it was. There are quotas now because of diminishing stocks. It can take years to get a licence for your own boat, and places on someone else's are almost impossible to find.

That's why I'm getting all the experience I can. And the money's useful too, cash in hand. Even if I do have to put up with Mackey's tall stories.

"The most famous thing that 'appened in Winchey Bay these last fifteen year was the lock-ins at the Ox and Plough," he was telling me. "Ah used to do a bit o' work as a barrel-trundler up at the Winchey Village brewery 'fore they shurrit down. That's 'ow ah'd knaa when they were ganna be. Ah'm tellin' yer man, us'd gan in there at six of a Sat'da neet an' not come out till Monday lunchtime."

"There used to be a brewery up Winchey?" I asked, before Mackey could begin the tale of some drunken exploit of his.

"Oh aye. They'd been brewin' on the Bay for more'n a thousand year. That's where the monks went after St Ninian's got sacked. They used to brew beer for the Bishop o' Durham."

"Yeah?" I wasn't sure if he was making it up or not. Were bishops allowed to drink beer? "Sounds like an easier way to mak' a livin' than fishin', anyweers."

"Oh aye. Ahways supposin' some Viking din't put a axe through yer 'eid." He gave a high-pitched laugh and chopped at the wind with his hand.

6

Larsen knew the sea and the weather as well as if he'd spent his whole life on the deck of a trawler. He had said the previous night that the storm would abate before dawn. No one else had shared his confidence, and so as the sun rose the *Shelty* was the only boat on the water as far as the eye could see.

He may have been regarded as unconventional by the other trawler captains, but I had seen too many of his predictions come true to doubt his knowledge of the elements. This was what I hoped to learn from him, and on every trip we took I tried to see why it was that he made the decisions he did. He was a quiet man and when I asked him directly he would often say nothing or just grunt and shrug. So instead I took to watching him, looking for the flaring of his nostrils, noticing the whitening of his knuckles on the *Shelty*'s wheel, and following the direction of his intent and frowning gaze. In this way I hoped eventually to be able to sniff the wind and know whether to expect fine weather or a storm, to feel the tug of the current on the rudder and be able to tell that the tide was about to turn, and to see a flock of gulls and guess from the way they screamed and tumbled whether or not they were worth pursuing.

On this particular morning, while he had been

right about the weather, Larsen seemed to have misjudged the best place to fish. We trawled back and forth across the mouth of Winchey Bay for an hour and a half without success. Each time we pulled in the net it contained nothing but driftwood and hanks of weed.

"Ah dinnaa why 'e's gannin' up the Sands," Mackey had said. "Storm'll've churned up the bottom ower much, ah reckon."

"Gan up off Lunny Head?" I suggested, after we'd hauled aboard another netful of rubbish. "At least it's rocky up there. We won't be pullin' out ahll this crap." I flung a barnacle-encrusted branch back into the sea.

Larsen stood in the *Shelty*'s stern, glowering down into the water. "Give it one more try," he ordered. "Further in this time."

I looked out across the rough, spray-flecked surface of the bay and could see no reason for his decision. I shrugged and began to prepare for the next cast.

This time I knew we had something as soon as the *Shelty*'s motor began to wind the net back towards the boat. You could always tell a full net from an empty one by the way the ropes hummed with tension from the weight of the catch.

"We've got something!" I shouted, springing to the gunwales to catch the first glimpse of what I hoped would be a boiling silver mass of fish rising from the waves.

"It's a tree," predicted Mackey gloomily. "Us've caught oursel's a tree."

The sound of the winch motor rose in pitch to an uncomfortable whine. The pulleys began to twist from side to side in a way I'd never seen before. I stared down into the sea. Our catch must be almost at the boat by now but there was still no sign of what it might be.

The winch reeled in a few more turns of rope. Beyond the floats that marked the mouth of the net we could now see a dense white cloud of frothing water.

"That's no tree," I muttered to Mackey. "Ah reckon this is ganna be our Christmas bonus!"

A fin like a scythe broke the surface. Then the *Shelty* rose on the swell and the net came up out of the waves. In it thrashed a single, huge black fish.

"Christ ahmighty!" shouted Mackey in panic. "It's a shark! Get rid of it quick!" He lunged for the quick-release lever that would detach the net from the winch.

Before he could reach it, Larsen knocked his hand away and began to swing the net over the deck of the *Shelty*.

The creature opened its jaws. The inside of its

mouth was ridged and grey and lined with rows of serrated teeth like jagged triangles of broken dinner-plate set in putty. It twisted its head and bit into the net, effortlessly shredding the mesh.

"What the hell are yer doin'?" croaked Mackey, his face pale. "Jus' lookarrim, man. 'E'll rip us in 'alf!"

The *Shelty* rolled again. The net swung inboard and the creature flopped out through the hole it had made and landed on the deck.

Whatever it was, it didn't look like any shark I'd ever seen a picture of. Its head was strangely heavy and blunt, and covered not with scales but with plates of bone or cartilage. These gleamed with an oily sheen like the carapace of a beetle, giving the enormous fish a masked or helmeted appearance of primitive ferocity. Its flanks were striped green and black like a giant mackerel. They slapped the deck with a wet and meaty sound, making the *Shelty*'s timbers shiver.

Mackey was dancing in the scuppers, trying to keep out of the way of the creature's thrashing tail. "'Irrit ower the 'eid!" he kept shouting.

Larsen had seized a boathook and was trying to get a good angle to land a blow. Seeing his chance he swung the long wooden pole but the creature rolled away. The blunt metal prong on the end of the boathook struck splinters from the deck.

Larsen staggered and nearly overbalanced on top of his catch.

The creature opened its mouth again and began to make an awful hissing, gurgling noise. I saw the black plates of bone over its throat move in and out as its gullet worked. *Thank God, it's dying,* I thought.

Seawater spewed from its gaping jaws. It retched again, coughing up more water and strands of greenish matter like half-digested seaweed. Then it arched its body and with a sudden whiplash movement catapulted itself over the gunwale and into the sea.

Spray sluiced over the three of us. Dashing the water from his face with his sleeve, Larsen leapt to the side of the boat. He stared down at the heaving waves, boathook at the ready, as if he thought he could snag the vanished fish with it and pull it back aboard.

Mackey was slumped against the *Shelty*'s winch, cursing under his breath. I saw him reach for his hip flask with white and twitching hands. Near him swung our ruined net, its torn mesh trailing over the side.

Larsen would be furious. There was almost certainly no way we could continue fishing today.

Picking my way cautiously through the mess left on the deck, I noticed something glittering in the pools of slime and seawater. I pushed at it with my foot. Then, all thoughts of the damaged net driven from my mind, I reached down to pick it up.

It was so heavy and slippery I nearly dropped it. Gripping it tightly, I plunged it into one of the buckets of water we kept ready for rinsing fish scales and blood from our hands.

No wonder the creature had nearly choked to death. There had been a golden serpent as long as my forearm lodged in its throat.

I shook the water from the shining sculpture and examined it more closely. It depicted a snake in the act of striking, rearing up with its teeth bared. The detail was extraordinary. An elaborate pattern of scales had been deeply etched into the serpent's sinuous body. A jewelled eye shone on one side of its head; there was an empty socket where the other should have been. Arching upwards from its back was a pair of wings inlaid with coloured enamel. One of the wings was damaged. It was bent out of true and many of the inlays were missing, exposing the fan-like framework of long, deep grooves in which they had been set.

I was turning to see if the others had noticed my find when Larsen loomed beside me. Before I could utter a word he had seized the statue and twisted it from my grip.

I opened my mouth but he stared me down, his

thunderous frown daring me to protest. Of course I hadn't been going to try and keep the find to myself. How could he act like I'd been going to cheat on my shipmates?

"Worrizzit? Is it gourld?" babbled Mackey, following Larsen aft. "Are yer ganna splirrit? It was ahll of us caught the thing y'knaa. That's fair, gan thirdies on it…"

Larsen stopped and turned to Mackey, a look of contempt on his face. "It's lost an eye," he said. "Why don't you see if you can find it?"

Mackey glanced uncertainly for'ard at the mixture of slime and water in the scuppers. As he hesitated, Larsen ducked into the wheelhouse and slammed the door. The sea frothed at the *Shelty*'s stern as he put the engine into gear.

It had only been two or three minutes since we had hauled our net aboard. Yet in that short time the weather had changed completely. The sandy beach and pine-covered slopes of Winchey Bay had disappeared in a bank of low-lying cloud. Out to seaward, instead of a clear view all the way to the horizon, there was nothing to be seen but a wall of roiling vapour. Even with the fog lamp switched on, visibility had shrunk to a few metres of choppy water.

The *Shelty* tilted steeply as Larsen put the helm hard over. Steering by compass, he set our course out of the bay. Tendrils of mist reached across the deck. The damp air clogged my throat, making me cough.

Larsen opened the throttle and the engine roared. From the way the timbers trembled beneath my feet I reckoned we must be going just about flat out. But oddly enough I felt only the gentlest of breezes on my face. Unladen, as she was now, the *Shelty* could make a fair rate of knots. On a calm day such as today she could feel as if she was skimming over the waves. But now she wallowed tiredly, and the wreaths of fog tumbled reluctantly over her deck.

Larsen leaned out of the wheelhouse. "She's sluggish," he shouted. "Check below to make sure we're not shipping water."

A hatch in the centre of the deck led down into the *Shelty*'s small hold. Kneeling, I slid back the wooden cover and peered below. It was immediately clear that the hold was dry. I was about to close the hatch again when a faint sound made me pause. Cocking my head to listen, I leaned further into the hold, straining my ears to hear above the rush of water along the hull.

There it was again: the noise of something scraping sternwards over the *Shelty*'s timbers.

I pushed myself upright. "Rocks!" I yelled, my voice cracking. "We're running aground!"

In the wheelhouse Larsen glanced down at the compass and shook his head. "Impossible!" he shouted back. "We're heading out into open sea…"

Once more the hold echoed to the sound of something rasping along the hull.

I ran for'ard and peered down into the waves. We might be ploughing through driftwood. It could be the stubs of snapped-off branches clawing at the keel like that.

Were there dark shapes moving in the water beneath the prow? I couldn't be sure. I turned back towards the wheelhouse. "Slow down!" I urged, thinking of the damage a fair-sized tree stump could do to the *Shelty*'s propeller.

Larsen ignored me. The clamour from the engine grew even louder as he tried to force more speed out of the struggling vessel.

Either he pushed it too hard, or something did indeed strike the propeller. Whatever the reason, before I could shout another warning the engine gave a loud bang and shuddered noisily to a halt, seized-up gear wheels screeching painfully.

A succession of feeble clicks came from beneath the engine cowling as Larsen vainly tried to restart the motor. The water hissed around us as the *Shelty* quickly lost what way she had.

From the wheelhouse I heard the sizzling of static. Then Larsen stepped out on to the deck. "Radio's gone haywire," he said. "Too much interference. Somebody break out the flares."

15

Fighting down my rising dread, I moved towards the cupboard where the emergency flares were stored. Running the *Shelty* at full throttle into a bank of fog was an act of recklessness I would never have thought Larsen capable of. It was a considerable risk to be adrift in these conditions. We would have to hope that the mist would clear and we could signal for help before the current swept us aground. I tried to work out which way the tide would be running. I looked at my watch but it had stopped and the glass had steamed over.

The *Shelty*'s Very pistol was kept wrapped in oilskin in a watertight box. I had watched Larsen himself check it less than a week ago. Yet now when I unwound the material a stream of icy water leaked out over my hands. The pistol and the flares it fired were waterlogged and useless.

Tired of waiting, Larsen was striding along the deck towards me. He still clutched the golden serpent tightly in one hand.

Silently I held the oilskin out towards him. He glared down at its soaking contents, his lips twisting under his bristling beard. Then he dashed the oilskin from my grasp. His eyes flashed with frustrated rage and his teeth gleamed yellow in the light of the *Shelty*'s fog lamp. I backed away from him. After two steps the gunwale was pressing against my calves.

Without any warning the deck shuddered beneath my feet and I was nearly tipped into the sea. Three tremendous blows struck the *Shelty*'s hull in rhythmic succession, rattling the glass in the wheelhouse windows and setting the door swinging on its hinges. I clung to a brass cleat for balance, pulling myself out of Larsen's reach as the boat rocked from side to side.

"It's that blurry black shark," slurred Mackey. "It's unnerneath us. It's ganna drag us ahll down wirrit." He had picked up the boathook and was swinging it this way and that. I flinched as he staggered and the blunt metal end of his makeshift weapon came dangerously close to my head.

One of you two's going to drown me, I thought. I imagined the history lesson I was missing, with Mr Aldwyn writing long lists of dates on the blackboard in squeaky chalk. I had been out at sea in thunderstorms and tearing gales, in mountainous seas and scouring blizzards, but this was the first time I'd ever wished myself back in the safety of my overheated prefab classroom.

We waited for a recurrence of the violent knocking. For what seemed like long minutes, nothing happened.

"Driftwood," I said at last, trying to convince myself. "Must've been a tree trunk or something. From the storm, or…"

"Listen!" interrupted Mackey, his voice hardly more than a croak. He was kneeling on the deck, his boathook jutting out over the gunwale like a lance.

I strained my ears and, sure enough, I could hear a noise. It was barely audible above the lapping of the calm sea, a distant crackle like the faint scrunching of newspaper.

"Summat's burnin'," muttered Mackey. "Smoke! Can yer smell it?"

I flared my nostrils and sniffed. It was true: the damp-laden air now had an acrid edge. At first I thought it must be the *Shelty*'s seized-up motor, but when I stretched out my hand to the engine cowling it was cold to the touch.

The sound of flames was becoming louder. And I now thought I could make out other noises too: the creak of timbers and the flapping of slack canvas.

I stared out into the mist. Was there a flickering light off the *Shelty*'s port bow? I couldn't be sure. My mouth was dry with fear. When I swallowed it felt like I was gulping down sand.

I turned away, perhaps subconsciously preparing to run. At my feet I saw the square black opening leading down into the hold. I had forgotten to replace the hatch. I recoiled, remembering the sounds I'd heard of something raking the hull.

Larsen moved for'ard, fists bunched defiantly.

"Ahoy!" he roared. "What ship goes there?"

The mist seemed to coil even more thickly about us. I stared into it until my eyes streamed. Sometimes I thought I saw glimpses of a high prow, a square-rigged sail and a long hull wreathed in smoke. The next moment the vision would seem to have been nothing more than a trick played on my eyes by the shifting vapour.

"There it is! Lookarrit! Ah, Jesus…" Hysterical, Mackey sprang to his feet and pointed into the mist.

"Get a hold of yourself, you old soak," Larsen snarled. "There's nothing there!"

Only terror could have given Mackey the nerve to defy Larsen. He had never before dared so much as to answer him back, yet now he stood his ground. Swinging his boathook up, he levelled the wavering tip at Larsen's chest.

"Throw it back. That snake thing. It's not yours. Throw it back."

Larsen raised his left arm, as if taunting Mackey with the golden statue. With astonishment I saw that it was no longer in his hand but entwined like a bracelet around his wrist.

"Don't interfere with me!" Larsen's voice was thick and hoarse. "It's mine. If you want it, come and take it!"

Almost weeping, Mackey screwed up his face and lunged wildly forward.

Larsen caught the end of the boathook. Swinging his shoulders, he wrenched it out of Mackey's hands. Thrown off balance, Mackey tumbled to the deck.

Now Larsen held the boathook. It hummed through the air as he turned, looking for me. I shrank away from him into the lee of the engine cowling.

I've never told a soul about what I witnessed then. Not even Mackey, who was face down and retching on the deck when it happened and never saw a thing.

I've tried a thousand times to persuade myself it must have been an illusion. That Larsen must simply have slipped and everything else was just my imagination. But the picture I have of that moment in my mind's eye seems too vivid not to have been real. When I concentrate I can see every tiny detail as if it was part of a photograph: the wet, white flesh tinged with green like a fish's belly; the ragged nails snagged with weed; and the thin, swollen-knuckled fingers adorned with a loose-fitting ring in the shape of a snake.

As Larsen stood at the *Shelty*'s prow, boathook raised like a club to strike anyone who dared approach, an arm came over the side of the boat, wrapped itself about his knees and dragged him into the sea.

The inquest returned a verdict of accidental death. The coastguards who rescued us had seen no signs of foul play. And neither Mackey nor I had stood to gain from Larsen's will. In fact he had left hardly any possessions: even the *Shelty* turned out to be mostly owned by the local building society.

The body was never found. A professor from a college in Newcastle gave evidence suggesting there was little point trying to look for it. He explained to the coroner how, in his opinion, the conditions off that part of the coast would make a search extremely difficult. For example, local records mentioned several interesting wrecks that had occurred in the vicinity, but attempts to find any traces of them had met with little success. The professor himself had organized diving expeditions in Winchey Bay, but had been defeated by the ever-shifting dunes and weeds that covered the seabed. All they had ever recovered were a few silver coins from a Spanish man-o'-war, and a piece of charred wooden timber from a Viking burial ship.

The Knock at the Door

Helen Dunmore

It's a fierce dark night with the wind tearing through it. We shouldn't be on the road at all, but it's Christmas time and we've got goods to sell. Dad's been sick for weeks. We've been laid up in Penzance in a small cold room which Mrs Nanjivey let us have out of kindness. Every night she came up with a shovelful of live red coals and laid it in the grate, and I put coal on piece by piece until there was none left. Mrs Nanjivey gave us what she could. Her man's away at sea, and she's got a baby downstairs to keep warm.

The coal ran out and there was no money to buy more. I went to sleep and dreamed I sat by a fire eating a pasty. The steak and potatoes steamed in rich gravy, but just as I opened my mouth to bite the dream stopped. Dad was coughing, and there was bread for breakfast. It lay cold and heavy on my stomach.

We had to get money. We had to get back on the road.

Our work is selling pots and pans, and mending them. We go from farm to farm and we give finest quality, fairest prices. When people have no money to buy new, Dad mends their pots and pans with his spitting-hot soldering iron.

The only thing I'm afraid of is the dogs. The ones that run mad on the end of their chains make me fear that one day they'll get loose and go for us. Some farmers keep their dogs loose anyway, to drive off strangers. But when they hear the chink of metal and see the bright flash of our cart full of metal pans coming over the hill they'll call the dogs off. They need us. Even the most tight-fisted farmer can't grow his own pots and pans.

Pots and pans for sale, finest quality, fairest prices, buy my pots and pans. Feel the weight, missus, you won't buy better.

Dad raps the pans to show the clean, clear ring of the metal. I bring out every size till the wife is suited. When the rain's lashing they let us in their kitchens sometimes. But I see them watching me sharp for thieving.

Sometimes a wife sets me down by the fire with a mug of hot milk and makes sure I drink it. That's 'cos I'm thin. But Dad tells them I'm strong enough, it's only that I don't pay for feeding. I could eat the old Queen's dinner and stay skinny. The old Queen eats plenty. She's fat and dressed in black, for she's been a widow more years than I can reckon. I've seen a picture of her.

At the farms they ask us for news of the roads we've travelled. Dad tells them his stories while I drink in the heat of the fire. They go nowhere off their own fields, these farming people, except to market in Penzance. I'd rather be me than them, except that they have a goose to kill for Christmas.

We left Penzance this morning and we've been on the road all day. We've been mending, not selling, apart from a little milk-pan a young wife fancied. Every farmer we speak to says it's been a bad year for him. But we've made enough for tomorrow's food and our lodging tonight, and Jimmy's. Jimmy's our horse. And the day after tomorrow is Christmas Day.

The mud's thick in the lanes and Jimmy's dead-tired with dragging the cart through it. He's getting old, Dad says. He won't do another winter with us. Me and Dad strain to push the cart when it gets stuck, and that sets Dad coughing again. I tell Dad to get in the cart and I'll walk alongside to ease the weight for Jimmy.

I've been walking many miles, but I'm strong. Dad gave me the rest of the bread with a bit of cheese. Being sick takes away his hunger.

It's a wild night and I think Dad's worse, not better. He's set the lantern on the front of the cart and as the wind blows it, so the light lurches from side to side like something living. It makes shadows that scare me more than the roaring dark.

Suddenly Jimmy puts his head down and shivers all over.

"This horse is near finished," cries Dad over the noise of the wind, and he clambers down off the cart to ease the weight further. We walk on, but soon Dad's coughing bad, doubled over. And I'm frightened. Dad needs food and a fire. He needs shelter.

"Dad, we can't go on."

Dad's breathing whistles worse than the noise of the wind. "We'll look for a barn, Mary. I'll be right again tomorrow. Look for a light."

But we are still dragging uphill. When we get to the top I'll maybe see a light. If it wasn't for the rain and wind in my face I'd see better.

"Dad! Over there!"

Dad shakes his head to clear it.

"There, Dad! There's a light."

"I don't recall a farm down there," says Dad.

"It's a strong light, look."

And indeed the light is strong. It seems to be shining just for us, across the wildness. Surely they won't turn us away on a night like this.

"All right, girl. We'll try it."

We splash and stumble off the lane and down a steep, narrow track between high granite hedges. The cart bounces and judders beside us. Jimmy's picked up speed. Maybe he knows there's a light, and if he's lucky a warm barn and hay.

"Steady there now, Jimmy."

We round the bend in the lane and there's the light again, full and strong. It's a farm, or maybe more than a farm. A big, royal-looking building with many windows set deep in the granite. A lantern on the gate, a lantern over the door, and light streaming out of all the windows. Rich folk who can waste light. You would think they were expecting us.

"Knock on the door, Mary, while I hold Jimmy's head. Steady now!"

There's a heavy iron knocker on the door. I lift it and it bangs down, booming. I wait for the bark and snarl of guard-dogs but it doesn't come.

The door opens, and a tall woman in a long black dress stands there. She has lace on her collar and the dress is silk. No farmer's wife dresses like that.

"Missus, madam, we're looking for shelter. My father's sick and we can't get as far as Pendeen.

26

Any barn or outhouse would do us."

She stands and stares at me.

"You're looking for shelter?"

"Yes."

"You're tired? Cold? Maybe hungry?"

"Yes, missus."

She sighs deeply. She calls behind her into the hall, "Strangers, Antony. They want shelter. They are cold and hungry."

When the man comes he's tall, too, and dressed in rich black. He looks at me keenly, as if I'm gold.

"Why are you here?" he asks, even though she's just told him.

"I'm – we're looking for a barn to stay the night, until the storm blows out."

"Ah," he sighs, like her, as if I've given him what he wanted. "And that's your father out there with the horse."

"We can sleep anywhere. We'll be no trouble."

"Fetch me my cloak, Susanna, and a lantern to light the way to the stable."

Then he bends down to me. "But you must come in the house. It's Christmas time and the wind is cold."

His face troubles me. It's so hungry, so deeply-scored with lines I can't read. You learn to read faces when you're on the road, but I can't read him. Antony.

"I must stay with my dad," I say. "He's sick."

"He'll come in too, once the horse is stabled."

My dad says yes, I'm to go in with Susanna while Jimmy's stabled. "We've fallen into heaven," Dad whispers, and he winks at me. Susanna takes me inside but I won't walk over their floor in my boots. My cloak hem is thick with mud as well.

"Take them off," says Susanna. "I'll put them to dry in the kitchen and in the morning we'll brush off the mud."

Once my boots and cloak are gone there's no running away. Already the heat of the house is stealing through me, and there are rich, spicy scents of cooking. I feel like Dad, as if I've fallen into heaven. There's a long, fine wooden table in the kitchen, but there's no food on it. Susanna leads me back into the hall, which is as big as a room, and sets me down on a stool by the fire. And then the door opens again and it's Dad, blinking in the light.

Me and Dad sit by the fire side by side on our stools, and Susanna and Antony leave us.

"This is a fine place," Dad says, looking around. "But I'd rather be at peace in the barn."

I know what he means. What are Susanna and Antony doing? Why are they so glad to see us? Through the kitchen door we can hear the chink of pans.

"God help us, they're making our Christmas dinner," says Dad.

Susanna comes in with a mug in each hand. I have milk, sugary and hot and spiced with cinnamon.

"I've made you a drink of horehound," she says to Dad. "It'll ease your chest."

"My mother used to say horehound was the thing for coughs," says Dad, taking the drink and sipping it. The fire is putting colour into his skin.

"I was only saying to Mary that we had fallen among the angels."

"Oh no," cries Susanna, starting back like a horse that's scared. "Oh no, don't say that! You don't know us."

"That's the root of it," Dad agrees. "You don't know us and we don't know you. And yet you treat us like royal kings."

"Oh no," says Susanna again, putting out her hand as if to stop Dad's words. "Don't say that." Her hand is shaking.

"A queer pair," says Dad when she's gone back into the kitchen. "Living alone between four walls sends people queer, Mary, and don't you forget it. It's only one night for us, but a lifetime within these four walls for them."

He looks better. Really better. The horehound drink has worked. Maybe he'll sleep all night without coughing.

"Even if we haven't fallen among the angels,

we've surely fallen on our feet," says Dad, and winks again.

"Mary?" says a voice. I jerk awake. No, I wasn't asleep. Just tired, in the heat of the fire. "Mary?"

"Where's my dad?"

"He's in the dining room. There's dinner ready for you, Mary."

Dining room? I stumble up from the stool. I have never been in a dining room before, though I know what it is. Rich people have a room for everything. A room for sleeping, a room for eating, a room for cooking. Even a room for reading sometimes, Dad says, if they are scholars.

"Come, Mary, this way," says Susanna. Her voice is timid and gentle. She acts as if I am the queen of this house, and she is the servant.

The dining room makes me catch my breath. It is full of dark, high furniture. The table is long and dark as a pool in the bog, and it shines like water. There are fine plates and silver knives and forks and a big branching silver candlestick. I can't count the burning candles, there are so many. But there are only two places laid. Dad is sitting at one end of the long table.

"Sit down, Mary, opposite your father," says Susanna. I glance at Dad as I sit down and he gives a small shrug of his shoulders.

Don't ask me what's going on, Mary, for I don't know, says the shrug.

The door swings back and a great golden-brown roast goose comes into the room, so big that at first I can't see the dish it's laying on, or Antony carrying it. A fat goose, with its skin stretched and crackling. There are roast potatoes, and stuffing, and bread sauce, and smoking-hot gravy. There's a dish of shiny carrots and a dish of roast onions. There's cabbage and roast parsnips and roast chestnuts.

Antony carves and Susanna asks what we'd like and serves us. I wonder if I can ask her later for some of the goose-fat to rub on Dad's chest. Goose-fat heals a cough.

"There," says Susanna, when our plates are full. She stands back, behind my chair.

The taste of the goose floods my mouth. I've never eaten goose-meat before. This is what the farmers have at Christmas, this is why they live between four walls, in their houses. Creamy bread sauce, crunchy, salty potatoes, sweet carrots. I eat everything Susanna has heaped on my plate, and when I've finished I wipe my plate carefully round with bread until it is perfectly clean. Dad's still eating, slowly, as if he's not hungry.

"Don't you like the goose?" Susanna asks him. "Would you prefer something else?"

"Didn't I tell you we'd fallen into heaven?" says Dad. "This is the food of angels, but my stomach's bad with the cough, so if you'll excuse me I'll take no more."

"Pudding?" Susanna asks me.

I've eaten nothing like this meal before, and my stomach is starting to hurt, like Dad's. I shake my head. If only I could take the pudding with me and eat it one morning when all we've got is cold bread. I can smell the spiciness of the pudding but I can eat no more.

"But you enjoyed it? You feel better now?"

"Thank you missus, madam," I say, and lay my knife and fork down on the table where I took them up.

"Best Christmas dinner I ever tasted," says Dad, but his plate is still three-quarters full.

"We've got your beds ready," says Antony, and this time it's Dad who starts back like a horse that's scared.

"We won't trespass on your house," he says quickly. "Mary and me'll be glad of a bed in the barn, that's all we need."

"But the beds are ready," says Susanna, and again her hand trembles as she lifts the plate.

"No, missus, we'll go in the barn and be glad of it," says Dad firmly, and my heart beats hard in relief. I don't want to sleep in these high, polished rooms. The fires are too hot and the Christmas goose lies heavy on my stomach. In the barn it'll be sheltered and sweet-smelling with straw and hay. We'll be safe there.

"Oh no," says Susanna, "please no. Stay here with us. Just for tonight."

"Yes, stay," says Antony, and he picks up the branch of candles and holds it high so that light splashes on the walls.

"If it's all the same to you, we'll be going," says Dad, and he comes around the table and grasps my hand. I've never been so glad of his touch.

"If it's all the same to you," says Dad again, "we'll make our way out to the barn. We'll not trouble you in the morning, we'll be on our way with Jimmy before you're awake."

They don't try to stop us, though I'm frightened they will. Susanna fetches my boots and cloak, which are warm and almost dry. She and Antony stand together, tall and straight in their rich clothes, with the smell of Christmas spices wreathing round them. We thank them again, but they say nothing. That's how I remember them, standing close together, Antony holding up the candlestick, his face scored heavy with grievous thoughts. And Susanna watching us with longing in her face.

In the barn I fall asleep at once, deep in my bed of straw, wrapped in my cloak. But I wake in the dead of night. The wind has dropped. The storm has blown away, and the moon is shining through the barn's high window. In its light I see that Dad isn't asleep. He's sitting up, watching, listening. Something about the way he watches makes me feel both safe and afraid. He is watching out for me, for both of us, against any danger. He's watching so I can sleep safe. I sink down and I'm dreaming again.

We leave early, at first light, as Dad said. Jimmy neighs and the cart clatters but no one comes out. The windows of the house stare blankly, as if no one's lived there for a hundred years. When we've gone all the way up the narrow, steep track and we're on the lane again, Dad says, "I'm not sorry to see the back of that place."

The farther away we get, the more cheerful Dad becomes. He begins to whistle, and Jimmy fairly springs along the lane.

"There's a likely-looking place," he says suddenly, as we reach a farm gate. "Let's see what we can do there."

Sure enough the farmer's wife wants a new pan to boil her puddings tomorrow. She makes us tea and Dad gets out his soldering iron to mend her tea-kettle. She even offers me an oatcake but my stomach is still heavy with roast goose.

"She had a fine big meal last night," Dad

explains. "We called for shelter at the big house along the lane. They treated us like king and queen, didn't they, Mary? The woman served us with her own hands."

"What big house?" says the farm wife, and I see her look, but Dad's bending to the soldering iron and he misses it.

"A couple of miles from here. A grand house with rows of windows. There can't be two of them."

"Were the lights burning?" asks the woman, and this time Dad hears the strangeness in her voice.

"A houseful of lights," he says. "You'd think they had lit them to welcome us. But they're neighbours of yours, you must know them."

"What did they look like?"

"Oh, fine rich people. She was dressed in silk and lace. And they were burning candles as if light was free as air."

"No doubt they want the light," says the farm wife sharply. "After all the darkness they've seen."

"You know them, then."

"I know their story."

And she tells us. Farm people can rarely tell stories like travelling people, but this story made Dad sit still with the iron going cold in his hand. And it made my heart turn inside me.

"I'm going back a way," says the farm wife. "It was a rough night, like last night, and just at

Christmas time as it is now. A man with a child came travelling along this lane. But the man was sick and sinking and he could go no farther. They saw a track and they saw a light shine, so he says to the child, "Go down there and ask for help and shelter." And the man wrapped himself in his cloak, sick as he was, and lay under a thorn bush in the storm for the child to come back with help.

The child went down the track to the house where the lights shone. He lifted the knocker, which was heavy, and struck the door with it. He heard the sound echo. But no one came, so he lifted the knocker again because he knew there must be people at home. Who leaves a house full of light? And he says he saw a face at one of the upstairs windows looking out at him, but still no one came.

It was a brother and sister who lived in that house. They had money and they wanted nothing and nobody but themselves. No one visited them and they visited no one. They had never opened a door to a stranger since their father died twenty years before, and they didn't open it now. The child knocked and knocked and he swore that he saw a woman's face looking out at him from the upstairs window, but no one came.

The child went back up the track and he spent the night wrapped in the cloak with his father, under the thorn bush in the rain and storm. In the morning they were found, but only the boy was living."

"Who found them?" I ask in a whisper.

"It was my great-grandfather who found them. He was a good man. If they had come here at first, they would both have lived, maybe. He kept the child with him, and when that boy grew up he married the youngest one of my great-grandfather's daughters. There were no sons."

"So he was your –"

"Yes," says the farm wife. "That child became my grandfather. He's dead now."

"But the brother and sister – Susanna and Antony – they're still living."

"No," says the farm wife, "they've been dead for more than fifty years. No one lives in that house now. But you're not the first to see them. It has to be a rough old night like last night. And Christmas time, with travellers. Those things don't come together often, but they do come. Fifty years they've been waiting there for a man and child to feed and shelter."

Dad sits back on his heels. "They asked us to stay," he says.

"No one's ever stayed," says the farm wife.

Much later, when we're rattling along behind Jimmy on the high road, I ask Dad what he

37

thinks. Will Susanna and Antony have to stay there waiting for ever? Dad frowns and twitches Jimmy's reins.

"Not for ever," he says at last. "They'll serve out their time and then they'll be free. She's haunted by that child who knocked at the door, you can see it in her eyes."

"But they're ghosts. How can they be the haunted ones, when they are the ghosts?"

"I don't know,' says Dad, "but that's the way it is."

"If we went back –" I say.

"No," says Dad. "Don't think of it, Mary. We're not going back."

But I do think of it, when the wind blows and the rain lashes and we're coming close to Christmas time again. I think of Susanna and Antony lighting all their candles so that a child will see the light. And waiting, waiting, waiting, for the iron knocker to lift and crash against the front door, so that this time they can open it.

No Man's Land

Susan Gates

Jake ripped open his last present. He'd been hoping against hope, even though it wasn't ball-shaped. When he saw it was a pair of gloves, his face scrunched into a scowl.

"Where's my football?" he said.

"What?"

Mum poked her head out of the steamy kitchen. It was only just after breakfast but she was already cooking Christmas dinner. She'd got up at six o' clock that morning to put the turkey in.

"My football," demanded Jake. "You said I'd definitely get one for Christmas."

"Did I?" said Mum vaguely, fanning herself to get some cool air. "It's like a sauna in this kitchen."

"I said I wanted one. And you promised."

"Did I?" repeated Mum, looking as if she had more important things on her mind.

"I told and told you," said Jake. He felt bad temper blooming inside him, like an evil flower. And he'd been in a great mood when he got up this morning! "I told you loads of times."

"I can't remember that," said Mum. She frowned suddenly. "I've still got those potatoes to peel."

"What was I supposed to do? Tattoo it up here?" Jake dragged a finger across his forehead. "Like, 'BUY JAKE A FOOTBALL'? I thought you were listening."

He made an ugly face at the gloves. They were woolly, from his great-gran. She probably knitted them herself. He wouldn't have minded a cool pair from a skateboarding shop.

"Stupid gloves." He chucked them across the room.

He knew he was taking a big risk. Mum wasn't the patient type at the best of times. But on Christmas mornings she could go off like a firework. That's what she did now.

"Don't you start!" she exploded. "You ungrateful brat! You've got loads of nice presents. And you're moaning about not having a football. You should be ashamed of yourself! Some poor kid in a refugee camp would give his right arm for those gloves!"

Jake opened his mouth to protest. He wanted to explain. How he'd already told his mates he was getting a football. How it was all arranged. In twenty minutes, they were meeting him at the field for a game. What were they going to say when he turned up without a ball?

"But Mum!" he said.

She gave him that killer shark glare. The one that could shrivel you up. It meant, "You think I'm giving you a hard time now? You haven't seen nothing yet. Any second now I'm going to blow like a volcano. Then you'd better run for cover."

Jake backed down. Better not upset her. Mum had the whole family coming for Christmas dinner. She'd probably already started on the sherry. Dad was keeping out of the way, down the shed.

Reluctantly, Jake clamped his mouth shut. Mum hung around in the doorway, still looking dangerous. But then a timer went off in the kitchen, PING!

"My sprouts!" shouted Mum, and she ducked back into the steam.

"Phew, those sprouts saved my life," said Jake, wiping imaginary sweat off his forehead.

It was no good. He was never going to get Mum to understand his bitter disappointment.

He stomped out the house, his shoulders hunched, and headed for the park.

"It's not fair!" he hissed through gritted teeth. He'd dropped loads of hints about that football. He'd even shown her the one he wanted in a shop window.

He gave a big sigh. "And I thought she was taking it all in," he said. There was a Coke can on the pavement. He gave it a vicious kick.

Mum had no idea what it was like. Every time he wanted a kick about, he had to wait for someone to turn up who had their own ball. That meant Bradley, who had about two brain cells. He always got the time wrong. He arrived after you'd got fed up and gone home. Or he went to the wrong place and waited for hours, wondering, *Why am I the only one here?* Or Harry, who was dead keen and always turned up right on time. But was absolute rubbish at football.

It was frosty. Ice sparkled on the pavement. Jake cupped his cold hands and puffed hot breath into them. He should have worn those Christmas gloves after all.

"Maybe they won't turn up," he thought, hopefully.

Fat chance. Two were waiting already. Stamping about to keep themselves warm. They had new football strips on.

They got what they wanted for Christmas, thought Jake.

Three others were straggling across the park. Lenny was using his mobile.

He's probably phoning my house, thought Jake, to say, *"We can't start without you. You're bringing the ball. Get your lazy butt out of bed."*

But that reminded him. He'd asked for a mobile for Christmas too. One of the latest models. But he knew he'd never get that, not in a million years.

At the last minute, he veered away from the field, dodged though some bushes. He just couldn't face his mates. It was too embarrassing.

"They'll think I was lying again," he told himself. Sometimes he did lie, saying he'd got things his Mum and Dad couldn't afford. He'd got into big trouble with that trail bike. "Yeah, my dad bought me it," he'd boasted. And, of course, they'd all begged, "Give us a ride on it!" He'd had to do even more lying, to get out of that one.

He felt sorry for himself. "All I wanted this time was one crappy football!" It wasn't like he was asking for the world.

He didn't want to go home yet. So he knocked on Great-Gran's door. She lived in the old people's bungalows, just outside the park. She looked surprised when he walked in. She was still in her dressing gown.

"It's not that time already, is it?" she said. "I thought your dad was picking me up at twelve."

"He is," said Jake, slumping into a chair. "I'm here on my own. Got any microchips?"

After he'd glugged red sauce on his chips and slotted a few into his mouth, he felt happier.

"Hey, thanks for the gloves," he told Great-Gran, grudgingly.

"Did you get some nice presents? Things you wanted?"

"I didn't get a football." He just couldn't help blurting it out. "And Mum practically promised me one."

"That's a shame," said Great-Gran, grieving along with him. Then her look brightened. "Wait a minute," she said. "I've got a football somewhere."

Jake stared at her, a microchip halfway to his mouth. "Have you?"

Magic, was his first thought. Then he thought again. "What kind of football?" he asked her, suspiciously. Great-Gran knew nothing about footballs. It was probably a little kids' blow-up beach ball. It was probably one she'd knitted.

"Oh, it's a proper one," said Great-Gran, as if she was reading his mind. She bustled out of the room. He heard her rummaging around in the cupboard under the stairs. "It belonged to your great-great-grandad."

"Who?" said Jake.

"My dad," explained Great-Gran, coming back with a dusty cardboard box. "I haven't looked at it for donkey's years."

She lifted it out of the box.

"It just needs pumping up a bit," she said.

Jake groaned. Why had he got his hopes up? It was a proper football all right. It was even made of leather. But it was a joke. It was the saddest, scabbiest, most scuffed football Jake had ever seen. He couldn't help grinning.

"Gran! It's a mess. It looks like a dog's been chewing it. I can't take that down the park. My mates would fall about laughing."

Great-Gran looked hurt. "Is it no good then? I suppose it is a bit old."

"How old?" asked Jake.

Great-Gran did some counting up in her head. "About ninety years old."

Jake burst out laughing. "Gran! It's as old as you. It's ancient. It ought to be on the Antiques Roadshow."

Great-Gran looked hurt again.

Just to please her, Jake pretended to be interested in the football. He took it from her.

"Ow!"

As soon as he touched it, a cold tingling feeling surged up his arms. When it reached the back of his neck, it made the hairs lift, like they do when you're scared. But what was there to be scared of? He was safe, here, in Great-Gran's bungalow. She even had an alarm, to call the warden.

Quickly, he put the ball down. He rubbed his tingling arms. He picked up his box of chips. But he couldn't shake off that strange feeling of dread. He even looked over his shoulder, as if there were someone hiding behind his chair.

"Put that ball away, Gran," he shuddered. "I don't want it. Put it back in the box."

But Great-Gran had gone all misty-eyed. She was caught up in memories. She'd got something else out the box. It was a tatty yellow piece of paper.

"This was the letter his mate brought back, when he came home on leave from the Great War."

"What war is that?" said Jake. His history was a bit hazy.

"It's the First World War I'm talking about," said Great-Gran. "Nineteen-fourteen to nineteen-eighteen. My dad was a soldier in that war. He fought the Germans. Except for Christmas Day, 1914. When he played football with them."

"Played football with the German soldiers?" said Jake, confused. "Weren't they supposed to be killing each other?"

"Not on Christmas Day," said Gran. "There was a truce."

She unfolded the letter. It seemed as fragile as a cobweb. She put on her reading glasses. Jake fidgeted. He'd suddenly got itchy feet. "Got to go now, Gran," he said.

Great-Gran took no notice. She pursed her lips, following the lines on the letter with her finger.

"There's some bits Dad wrote about the rats and the mud and the fighting and how awful it was in the trenches. But here's the part about that football game."

Gran read it, in a high warbly voice, sometimes stumbling over the words.

"The dawn was freezing cold and foggy at first. It was dead quiet, without the shells and the guns. My mates said, 'You're barmy.' I don't know what made me do it. But I just stood up on the parapet and no one shot me! So I took my football and went out into No Man's Land. I saw Fritz poking his head above his parapet so I gives the ball a kick and says, 'Fancy a game, Fritz?' and blow me someone says, 'OK, Tommy.' And they all comes trooping out, real friendly. We even shake hands, like we hadn't been blasting each other to kingdom come the day before!"

Great-Gran stopped reading. She folded the letter up again.

Jake jumped to his feet. "Can I borrow that ball, Gran?" He'd forgotten how even touching it had spooked him, seconds ago.

Great-Gran looked surprised, "I thought you didn't want it."

"Yeah, but that was before. Before I knew my great-great-grandad was a soldier. And that he had a kick about with some Germans on Christmas Day. I want to show my mates. This football is famous!"

He scooped up the ball. Again that chilly shiver ran up his arms. As if some kind of connection were being made. But he hardly noticed. He was more excited now than scared.

"Can I have the letter too?" He reached out to take it but Great-Gran drew it back.

"I think I'll keep it here," she said.

For a second Jake was indignant. Great-Gran never said no. She always let him have anything he wanted. "Why?" he frowned.

"Because I don't want nothing to happen to it. I told you, Dad's best mate brought it back for his family, along with this football and some of his other things. My dad never got the chance to post this letter," said Great-Gran, her face suddenly filling with sadness. "He got shot. Boxing Day, 1914, when I was just a baby."

"Wow!" said Jake, excited. "So that letter got found on his body? Are those bloodstains?" This was going to make a great story to tell his mates. They might even forget that he hadn't got a new football.

"Catch you later, Gran."

Leaving Great-Gran still lost in her memories, he went speeding up the path. He was pleased to be outside. It was too hot and stuffy in Great-Gran's house. After about twenty minutes talking to her, he always wanted to escape.

He raced back to the park, with the football under his arm. Were his mates still there? Some had gone home. But three or four were still hanging around, their breath making white clouds in the frosty air.

"Hey, you guys, guess what I've got?" he shouted.

The faces they turned towards him weren't welcoming.

"So you decided to turn up," said Lenny, sarcastically. "We've been freezing to death, waiting for you. You said ten o clock."

Jake held out the football, "I've got this, though."

There was dead silence. Then someone hooted with laughter. And Lenny said, in disgust, "You trying to be funny or what? You keep us waiting for ages. Then you turn up with that?"

"No, no," said Jake, struggling to explain. "You don't understand. It's not to play with. It's an antique. I just bought it to show you. It's a famous football. My great-great-grandad, he was a soldier. Right? And he played a game with the Germans, with this football, in the First World War."

"So?" said Lenny, still in the same sarcastic voice.

49

And someone else said, "Does that mean you didn't get a new football? Just like you didn't get that trail bike? So you're making up some kind of stupid lie. About a famous football or something?"

"Yeah," added Lenny. "Look at the state of it. He probably picked it out of a skip on the way here."

"I didn't. I didn't," spluttered Jake, his face turning bright red. "And I'm not lying."

But they were already walking away. They didn't once look back. They disappeared through the big, iron gates. There was no one else around, not even dog-walkers. He was alone, in an empty park, on a frozen football field.

Suddenly, the football felt as heavy as a boulder in his arms. Jake dropped it on to the grass. Why had he brought it to show them? He must have had a brainstorm. He should have known they'd just make fun of it.

"Stupid football." He gave it a kick.

There was no chance of a game now. He had no one to play with. He shivered and hugged himself. It was getting colder. The kind of cold that went right through to your bones.

"Might as well go home," he muttered to himself.

Fed up, he gave the football another boot.

There was a strange mist creeping towards him

across the grass. Where had that come from? It curled and writhed like snakes. It lapped around his shoes in creamy waves.

Suddenly, he realized he'd lost the football. The mist had swallowed it. That football was a family heirloom. Great-Gran would go mad!

But the mist was rising, getting thicker. First the trees were fuzzy black shapes. Then they vanished altogether. Now, there were white cotton-wool walls closing in on him. Jake blundered about in the fog, his sense of direction totally scrambled.

"Aaargh!"

He was teetering on the edge of a big crater. His arms whirled like windmills. He saved himself, just in time, from slithering down the sides. What was that doing there? There should be barriers to keep kids from falling in. There should be signs saying, "DANGER. KEEP OUT."

The bottom was full of slushy mud. It looked like lumpy, yellow porridge.

"You could drown in there!" Jake gasped, horrified.

And, if anyone heard your cries for help, in this fog they wouldn't be able to find you. When he stretched out his arm, he couldn't even see his own fingers, waggling in front of his face.

He stumbled into a muddy rut. It had frozen, hard as iron. What had happened to their football field? It hadn't been smooth before. But now it was like a construction site.

Where am I? thought Jake. He didn't know this part of the park. He felt scared, totally disorientated.

"You've got to get out of here," he told himself. "Find the park gates." Even a bench, or a litter bin would be something familiar.

Then something rolled slowly towards his foot. His toe stopped it. He looked down. It was the football, lying in an icy puddle. Someone had just kicked it back to him.

Those hairs on the back of his neck weren't just lifting now. They were wriggling about, like maggots.

"Who's there?" he shouted, trying to peer through the smoky swirls. Maybe one of his mates had come back, looking for him.

"Who's there?" he shouted again. "Is that you, Lenny?"

His eyes screwed up. What was that? He could see twinkling lights in the fog. A row of twinkling lights, floating high up above the ground.

"What's happening?" Jake thought, panic-stricken. "What is this place?"

Then a voice drifted through the freezing, foggy air.

"Merry Christmas, Tommy!"

My name's not Tommy, thought Jake, bewildered.

He stumbled into something. It was a bunch of tunic jackets, some khaki, some grey, piled up in a heap. There was another heap over there. He could just make it out, through the haze.

He and his mates often piled up their hoodies and jackets like that.

It looks like ... goalposts, thought Jake, frowning.

"Pass that ruddy ball, Fritz!"

Without thinking, Jake reacted. He booted the ball. Instantly the fog around him was full of running figures. The ball came back to him.

Jake started running too. But he kept the ball at his feet. He booted it again. It curved off into the mist. The figures around were keeping up with him. He was in a football game! He couldn't see faces, only shapes. But they were laughing, shouting, skidding on ice.

"Over here!" shouted Jake wildly, all flushed and excited. And someone passed him the ball. With a mighty kick, he belted it back into the fog.

"Goal!" someone yelled. "Well done, Tommy!"

Hey, thought Jake. *I'm doing good here.*

"Look out, Jake!"

Who'd shouted that? It was an English voice. It came out of the fog and stopped him pitching head-first into another huge crater. He flung himself down, just in time, at its icy edge. But he slid forward so he was almost overhanging it, staring into its depths.

"No!" There were things floating in the mud. He didn't want to look. An arm sticking out, a boot. The back of someone's head. There were dead soldiers down there!

Jake scrambled up. He thought, *I'm gonna be sick*. His legs felt as wonky as a newborn foal's.

Then, out of the fog, Great-Great-Grandad's football trickled gently towards him. It stopped at his feet.

Suddenly, he found the strength to run. He snatched up the ball and hared off. Soon, he was on smoother ground, dodging through the fog, slamming into trees and park benches. Until he was hanging, half-hysterical, on to the park gates, gasping for breath, his heart hammering.

"You all right, son?" said someone. It was an old guy, walking his dog.

Jake could hardly speak. He pointed a shaking finger. "Out there! Out there! Look!"

Together, they stared into the park. The fog had gone. There were only a few wispy rags left.

"What you on about, son?" the man said.

"Can't you see?" screamed Jake. "It's No Man's Land!"

But No Man's Land had gone too. The litter bins, benches, and trees were back. The park looked just the same as it always did. Except the sun had come out over their football field. Making the ice crystals on the grass sparkle like jewels.

His brain numb, Jake trudged back to Great-Gran's, carrying the football. He couldn't think, daren't think, about what had just happened. And what he'd seen.

The ball was soggy now, heavy to carry. It made his arms ache.

Jake plodded wearily into Great-Gran's living room.

"Take those shoes off!" said Great-Gran straight away. "You're making a right mess of my carpets!"

Dazed, Jake looked down. His trainers were caked with thick yellow mud. There was no mud that colour round here.

"Where've you been?" fussed Great-Gran. "In a mud bath? Look at your clothes. Your mum's going to have a fit."

Jake slumped into a chair.

"Here's your ball back," he said to Great-Gran. He wiped some mud off it with his sleeve. Then put it gently on the coffee table.

"You know," said Great-Gran, "after you'd gone, I had a proper read of Dad's letter. Would you believe it, them Germans put up trees at

Christmas? On top of their trenches, all among the barbed wire? They even lit candles on the branches. They looked real pretty, Dad said, twinkling through the morning mist."

"I saw them," said Jake, speaking as if he was in a trance. "And we played football. And someone knew my name, Gran. Someone called out to warn me."

"What, my pet?" said Great-Gran, looking totally baffled.

Jake sighed. He shook himself like a wet dog.

"Never mind, Gran," he said. "I'm just talking rubbish."

Had he really played football with ghosts in No Man's Land? And had his own great-great-grandad called out to him? To save him from falling into a shell hole full of corpses?

He shivered. His brain couldn't cope with that. Best not to think about it. Block it right out of his mind. Pretend it never happened. But there was one thing to say before he did.

"Put that football back in the box, Gran," he begged. "And don't take it out again, ever."

"I'll buy you a brand new one, pet," offered Great-Gran, shutting the ball away and closing the box lid. "You can come with me. Show me which one you want."

"Thanks, Gran," said Jake, pleased.

"But we won't be able to get it until the shops open, after Christmas."

"That's OK," Jake told her. "It's not that important. I can wait."

Lady in Blue, Unidentified

Terence Blacker

I write this report on Christmas Day in the library of Oxburgh Hall, an agreeable late-medieval moated house in Norfolk where I have been a guest for these past five days. By the end of this week, I am confident that my task will be complete.

The vampires will be dead.

No, please don't be alarmed. I shall not, in these pages, be taking you into the spooky world of heebie-jeebies and hobgoblins. It is the myth of the vampire that I am here to slay – the farrago of fictional nonsense (fangs! long cloak! crazed blood lust!) that shall be destroyed by the oldest weapon known to man.

Reason. Logic. Our old friend, common sense.

Because, although I earn my living from writing books for children (for telling tales *in* school, as it were!), I am essentially a man of fact.

So when the publishers of this volume, Scholastic, challenged me to write a story that would disprove the existence of vampires, I was tempted. When that firm's editor Mr Forder told me that I would be required to spend a week over Christmas at the famous tourist haunt, Oxburgh Hall, I needed no further encouragement. I have never been an enthusiast for the so-called "yuletide" festivities and the chance of escaping the season of jingle-bell mummery and flummery by doing some research in an agreeable country house – and being paid for the privilege – was too good to miss.

You see, I cannot abide superstition; the so-called "paranormal" is, in my humble opinion, nothing more than clutter. Pointless mental clutter.

And yet, as I learnt when arriving here by taxi from Downham Market station, these ancient fears persist.

The taxi-driver, having accepted my fare, cast one glance at Oxburgh Hall, with its dim lantern hanging outside the gatehouse, a pale, wintry moon glinting on the moat, and shuddered. "You wouldn't catch me staying there over Christmas, mate," he muttered. "Talk about a spooky atmosphere." And before I could point out that, without an atmosphere (i.e. the gaseous envelope of oxygen and nitrogen around Planet Earth), we would all be in trouble, he had driven off, leaving me alone, my suitcase beside me, outside the great house.

Whistling, I crossed the small bridge to the gatehouse where I found, by the porter's lodge, a small doorbell. I pressed, and a distant tintinnabulation could be heard from the dark recesses of Oxburgh Hall.

No lights came on. There were no distant footsteps from within the house, nothing to break the unearthly silence – not even (I jest) the sound of vampiric bats unfolding their wings! I pressed the bell again, and waited.

After a couple of minutes, I left my suitcase by the gatehouse and wandered into the courtyard. By now my eyes were accustomed to the darkness, and for a moment I took in the magnificence of the house which, illuminated by the moonlight, surrounded me. Even to one normally blind to architectural beauty (my family accuses me of being "artistically impaired"), the Hall was an astonishing sight.

For five centuries these buildings had belonged to the Bedingfeld family, apart from a brief period in the eighteenth century when the house had been occupied by a Sir Edmund and Lady Challoner. It was around certain unhappy domestic events during these years that a wild vampiric mythology had grown.

"Mr Blacker?"

The voice, from behind me, interrupted my thoughts. I turned quickly, startled that someone could have appeared at the gatehouse without my hearing his approach. Standing by the door was a tall, broad figure, holding my suitcase.

"Apologies," he said, in a voice that seemed somehow too frail and reedy for his size. "I was in my room in the East Wing."

I stepped forward and introduced myself.

"My name is Gilbert Franck," he said. "I am the caretaker."

"I'm relieved to see you, Mr Franck." I smiled. "For a moment I thought I'd been abandoned to the vampires of Oxburgh."

Laughing, we entered the Hall by a small door to the left of the gatehouse. As he led me up some winding stairs, it occurred to me that the reason why stories had spread of a supernatural presence at the Hall lay in the peace (gloom would be too strong a word) of the building itself. We made our way down a corridor before Franck opened a door, announcing, almost like an old-fashioned butler, "Your room, Mr Blacker."

The bedroom in which I now stood was neither grand nor baronial, but a homely little affair with a low, sloping ceiling and a small window overlooking the moat and garden. It had once been a nursery, Franck informed me.

"I shall be serving dinner within fifteen minutes," Franck said. "You'll find the dining room across the courtyard beyond the gatehouse."

"Dinner? Nothing elaborate, I hope."

"I like to cook."

He certainly did. To my pleasure and astonishment, I was treated to a three-course meal by candlelight in the panelled dining room.

As I partook of the excellent vegetable soup, Franck revealed that he had indeed once been a chef. Since his retirement, he had been employed part-time to look after the property during the closed season when no tourists visited.

"Retirement?" I looked up from my soup in some surprise. "Forgive me, but you seem rather young to retire."

Franck inclined his head graciously. "I'm older than I look," he said. "And unfortunately I have a rather delicate heart. My doctor advised me to escape the hurly-burly of the kitchen in favour of a less stressful occupation."

I observed that I looked forward to enjoying his culinary skills over Christmas dinner.

My remark seemed briefly to disconcert the caretaker. "We do not celebrate Christmas at the Hall," he said quietly.

"A man after my own heart," I chuckled. "It is

one of life's mysteries why the world goes collectively mad at this time of the year."

"Mad, yes. It is indeed." Franck smiled, as if amused by a private joke, then changed the subject of conversation. "Presumably you'll be concentrating on the story of Margaret Challoner while you are here."

"Yes. A week among the private papers, and I'll be able to put the famous vampires to rest for good and all."

"You seem remarkably confident, Mr Blacker."

"Of course I'm confident. You see, demystifying the so-called 'paranormal' is something of a hobby of mine. I've already proved to my satisfaction that the original werewolves were nothing more than hungry wolves who were seen by gullible villagers digging up graves for food. As for all those stories about 'ghosts' arising from graveyards, it's clear to me that they were simply the bacterial glow – *protobacterium fisheri*, it's called – produced by the decomposing flesh of corpses. Of course, vampires are rather more complex."

So, as I was served my main course – some marvellous poultry dish – I expatiated upon my latest theory.

The myth of the vampire, or *vrykolaka* as it was known in Romania, dated back to the plague. At that time, there was naturally an almost hysterical fear of death. Stories of ghosts tormenting entire villages. Bodies were disinterred, examined. And what was found? Sometimes there was blood around the corpse's mouth. Its flesh seemed alive. When cut, blood still flowed.

"And science has an explanation for all these phenomena?" asked Franck.

I smiled. "Of course it has. Victims of the pneumonic form of the plague frequently bled around the mouth after death. As the lungs and viscera of the body expanded, blood was forced upwards towards the mouth. In the cases of sudden deaths – which were said to have caused vampirism – the abrupt removal of oxygen from the bloodstream frequently meant that it wouldn't coagulate after death. Hence the running-blood theory."

"What about the fangs and the long black cloak?" Franck stood up and filled my glass with wine. "What about red-eyed creatures feasting on the jugular?"

"Pure fiction. As it happens, traditional vampires were said to feast on the heart," I said. "It was Bram Stoker whose feverish imagination dreamt up the fangs and the neck idea. Before Count Dracula, the folkloric vampire was thought to be a bloated, ruddy-cheeked individual – a putrescent, walking corpse in other words."

Through my discourse, Gilbert Franck had listened politely but now he seemed to wince queasily.

"How is the swan?" he asked.

"Swan?"

"I cooked swan for you tonight."

I laughed appreciatively. Teachers and critics have been kind enough to comment on the "humour" of my stories, and I was glad to find that the caretaker was no stranger to zaniness himself. "Yes, the *swan* was excellent, thank you very much."

Later, well-fed but tired, I made my way across the courtyard and upstairs, having bid my host a very good night.

So this was a haunted house! To tell the truth, I had rarely felt more at home. Why, even the bed into which I slipped seemed warm and welcoming.

Only once that night was my rest disturbed. Some time in the early hours, I was awoken by a soft weight upon my chest. It appeared that a house cat had adopted me. I smiled in the darkness before drifting off into the deepest of slumbers.

The sleep of the dead, you might say.

No research can have been accomplished in such agreeable circumstances as was mine during the first part of my week at Oxburgh Hall. Rising at eight, I would be treated to one of Gilbert Franck's superb cooked breakfasts. Then to the library for a morning amongst the family papers. Light lunch in the Saloon, more work, a brief constitutional around the garden, and a final session in the library. The day would end with a candlelit meal, with the excellent Franck waiting in attendance.

It is no exaggeration to say that quite soon I had begun to feel as at home as any lord of Oxburgh Hall might have done. In fact, such was my natural authority that Franck had taken to calling me "sir" and generally behaving as if he were my faithful servant.

I did not correct him – indeed I'm ashamed to say that I discovered I have a taste for being in authority and was rather good at it!

My research, too, was most satisfactory.

The years from which the vampire myth had originated were – perhaps unsurprisingly – ill-documented in the Bedingfeld family papers, but fortunately a local rector, the Reverend Herbert Radcliffe, had recorded events of that time in his diary.

Grief-stricken by the death of his young wife Mary, the fourth baronet Sir Richard Bedingfeld had, in 1767, sent his son to London to be educated by nuns and had himself entered a monastery to become a virtual recluse for the next five years.

During that time, according to Radcliffe, a man called Sir Edmund Challoner, a merchant and fellow Catholic, had been allowed to use the house. Challoner spent most of his time in Norwich, leaving his wife Margaret ("a miracle of young comeliness, as spry and gay as a sparrow," said Radcliffe) at Oxburgh Hall with their young son Edward.

This, it transpired, had been unwise. In 1769, Radcliffe's diary reported "a tragick vexation at the Hall".

For some months, there had been noisome rumours in the village, viz. that her ladyship had developed an unseemly affection for Joshua Spiers, a member of the household retinue. Often were the times, according to loose tongues, that her ladyship released her servants from their duties early in the evening, leaving her alone with Spiers and her son, the young Edward. Further improprieties, which it will not be beyond the wit of my readers to imagine, were imputed by local gossips to the young couple.

Whether the word of such outrages reached the ear of Sir Edmund I know not, but the facts of his unhappy discovery are as clear as water. On the night of December 21st, he returned early for the Christmas season to find his wife and Spiers at sport in the Great Hall. Overcome by an intemperate rage – my hand hesitates to record such enormities for posterity – Sir Edmund seized a carving knife from a table nearby and slayed the unhappy couple.

The tragedy was not yet over. The following morning, servants found Sir Edmund hanging by the neck from a rope attached to a beam in the Great Hall.

Wandering amidst this unhappy scene was the poor little Edward, no more than nine years of age, so distracted with grief and confusion that be was struck quite dumb.

A messenger brought me post-haste to the house where, the bodies having been made decent and laid out in a ground-floor bedchamber, I pronounced the Office of the Dead upon the three of them.

While we were thus occupied, Edward was seen to walk in a trance out of the house. His body – the final horror – was found in the moat, face down, staring into the murky depths of the water and, I fancy, of the human heart.

God rest their unhappy souls.

"Would you care for some tea, sir?"

I looked up from Radcliffe's diaries to find Gilbert Franck standing before me. I had been so absorbed in the Reverend's account that I had failed to hear him approaching.

"So that was why Sir Richard destroyed the Great Hall," I said quietly.

"It is possible, sir. No other explanations have been offered for such a drastic step."

I shivered. "It's a Christmas story with a difference."

"A true Christmas story, sir."

"Yes, of course. All fact." I closed the book and stood up. "Fact is always somehow more disturbing than fiction."

And I *was* disturbed. After tea, I walked by the moat, turning over in my mind the details of the Reverend Radcliffe's account. So deep in thought was I that I soon found myself by the small chantry chapel, which was almost concealed by trees on the far side of the drive. It was from there, as the evening gloom closed in on me, that I heard the sound of a human voice, female, singing quietly.

Approaching stealthily, I saw, seated upon a small stone tomb, a woman, dressed in a long, blue velvet dress. As she sang some kind of lullaby to herself, she swayed backwards and forwards, almost like the trees buffeted by the winter wind.

From my vantage point on the gravel drive, I could just see that the woman was working on some kind of tapestry. Quite suddenly, as if someone had called her, she stopped singing. Slowly, she turned to me, gazing through the trees.

That face, those features: they weren't pale and sad, as somehow I had been expecting, but almost comically dappled and rosy-cheeked.

She smiled, and the look she gave me was of such heart-stopping intimacy, such warmth, that, never having been what they call "a ladies' man", I found myself blushing. Without a word, I hurried back towards the house.

Franck was laying the table in the dining room.

"There's a woman by the chapel," I said, rather more loudly than I intended. "Knitting, singing. In the dark."

"That would be Miss Preston, sir," said Franck.

"Miss Preston?" I said angrily. "Who the hell is Miss Preston, and what is she doing on my – in the grounds?"

"A nanny, sir. She lives in a cottage, in the village. Retired." Something approaching a smile appeared on the caretaker's face. "You weren't thinking she was from … another place, sir?"

"Certainly not. It was just that, after reading all about the Challoners, it gave me a bit of a turn."

"Of course, sir."

I returned to the library, where Franck had thoughtfully lit a fire. I felt rather strange, with that peculiar heaviness that sometimes precedes a bout of flu. Sighing, I returned to my research, reading my way through the Reverend Radcliffe's diary for the year of 1770. There was, so far as I could see, a single reference to the tragic events at Oxburgh Hall.

On the fifth day of September I was considerably discomfited by a deputation of three servants from the Hall, requesting upon my doorstep that I should use my sacred offices to rid the great house of what they called "the curse of vampyres". In vain I argued with them that the work of the Lord's servant does not extend to the removal of imaginary hobgoblins, particularly from a Catholic household, and that this story was an insult to reason itself.

Yet their perturbation was so great that, out of sheer pastoral sympathy, I was obliged to listen to them as they told their tales of the vampyric presence of Joshua Spiers and Lady Challoner, who now, they averred, held Oxburgh Hall in their thrall. Sir Richard Bedingfeld, the servants said, had already succumbed, as had other members of the household. I was solemnly informed that, because no vampyre is invested with a knowledge of his own state, the afflicted continue to believe that they are normal members of the human race.

These then were their fancies. A week later, I called at the Hall during my tour of the parish. There I was told, by one of the very manservants

71

who had visited me the previous week, that all was well and that my services were no longer required.

Such are the strange byways of superstition among servant folk.

I leafed through the rest of the Radcliffe diaries, but there were no further mentions of "vampyres" or indeed of Oxburgh Hall.

Slowly, I laid the book back on the desk. Joshua Spiers and Margaret Challoner. "Because no vampyre is invested with a knowledge of his own state, the afflicted continue to believe that they are normal members of the human race." I walked out of the library to the West Staircase, where portraits of the family are to be found. All are named, except one. The fifth painting along is of a young woman, described in the guidebook as "A Lady in Blue, unidentified". Slim, pale, she was much smaller than the figure I had seen by the chapel, but there was something in those eyes. The blue dress was identical.

Back in the library, I found a book of household accounts. I turned to the year 1769. There, in the list of "manservants and maidservants" was the name which confirmed Radcliffe's account of the murders.

Joshua Spiers, Cook.

My limbs heavy from the approaching fever, I made my way out of the library towards the kitchen from where I could hear the sound of Franck preparing my evening meal.

"Sir?" The caretaker was standing at the kitchen table, basting what appeared to be a roast sucking pig. "Is something wrong?" His voice betrayed the mild disapproval of a servant whose territory has been encroached upon.

"A strange coincidence," I said, in as natural a voice as I could manage. "The lover of Lady Challoner was, like you, a cook. Funny, that. Something else. Near where little Edward Challoner drowned, I just happened to see a woman, singing to herself in the twilight. A lady in blue, unidentified."

Franck fixed me with those dark, expressionless eyes. "I fear you have lost me, sir," he said quietly.

"If I were the sort of person to believe in vampires – which I am not – I might be tempted to reach the conclusion that Joshua Spiers and Margaret Challoner were here, still alive, singing and –" my teeth chattered – "cooking my supper."

"But that wouldn't be fact, sir. That would be hocus-pocus."

"Precisely!" I said angrily. "The publishers who sent me here are so desperate to sell their books and encourage children in superstitious beliefs that they have set up little vampire games to fool me, a serious writer and researcher. It's … it's a scandal."

"May I venture to suggest that you are not well, sir."

"Yes, Franck. I have made up my mind. I shall not complete this commission." I glanced at my watch. It was five-thirty. "Today is the l ast working day before Christmas. I shall ring Scholastic right now and tell them of my decision."

I returned to the Saloon. As luck would have it, Forder was still at his desk when I called. He expressed concern for me in my flu-ridden state. Of course he understood if I had lost my enthusiasm for the commission. No, he wouldn't dream of allowing me to return to London by train, feverish and distressed as I was. In fact, he would drive down himself and collect me that very night. Would nine-thirty be acceptable?

It would.

In no condition to eat a meal, I tottered miserably back to my room and packed my case. I sat on my bed, exhausted by this exercise, and waited.

Suddenly the drowsiness which I had felt all day closed in on me as surely as the darkness outside the window. I lay back on the bed and shut my eyes.

When I awoke, it was with a start. I discovered, as I tried to sit up, that sleep had done nothing to ameliorate my fever. Looking at my watch, I cursed. Ten o'clock. Where the hell was Forder? Why hadn't I been awoken?

Unsteadily, I made my way downstairs. A low murmuring sound reached me from the direction of the dining room. Thank God. The publisher was here. Out of politeness, he must have refrained from...

A strange and singular sight awaited me in the dining room. At the table, seated close together, their features lit by candlelight, were two figures, one dressed in black and one in blue. Gilbert Franck and the woman I had seen outside, Miss Preston.

As I stood, swaying, at the door, they looked at me in silence. Then, in a voice that was somehow less respectful than I had come to expect, Franck said, "It seemed a shame to waste the sucking pig. Since you were indisposed, I invited Miss Preston for supper."

"I f-feel terrible. Where's Forder? He's late."

"Ah. Mr Forder rang. He has been unavoidably detained. He said something about a Christmas party, sir. He will collect you tomorrow."

"No." My legs felt weak and for a moment I felt as if I were about to lose consciousness.

"My lord –" The woman spoke for the first time. She seemed concerned on my behalf but, as she made to stand up, Franck took her hand as if to restrain her.

My lord? Why did she call me that?

And there, there in the guttering candlelight of the dining room, I looked and I saw. Two hands, one holding the other, both plump, soft, ruddy. In the swirling mists of semi-consciousness, I suddenly knew with terrifying certainty that this was no stunt. Before me stood the revenant forms of Joshua Spiers and Margaret Challoner, swollen, corpse-like vampires. And me? Why, it was obvious: I was their lord, Sir Edmund Challoner, doomed to act out my own death, trapped by – trapped by what?

"Forder." My own voice seemed distant, as if it belonged to someone else, speaking in another room. "It was Forder who was so keen that I should come to Oxburgh Hall." I tried to visualize the publisher. Big, yes, rosy-cheeked – but then, now I came to think of it, all the people I had seen at Scholastic had somehow seemed unfeasibly bonny, with a strange, bloated quality to them.

"Not the whole of Scholastic, surely?" It was a whisper, almost a death rattle in my throat. "They can't all be vampires. Not the editors. Not the managing director. Not –" my head spun at the horror of it all – "not the sales representatives travelling all over the country?"

"Bedtime, sir." Franck was standing now. "Perhaps I could bring you a hot—"

"No!" I backed away from the two of them, stumbling out into the courtyard, the sound of my sobbing breath roaring in my ears. I took the first steps on the stairs and stopped, suddenly aware that there was someone standing before me.

"Please, sir."

It was a child, a boy of nine or ten, dressed in a long, flowing nightgown. He seemed to be trying to tell me something, repeating, with a kind of hopeless desperation, the same phrase.

"Please, sir... Please, sir..."

"What d'you want?" I asked faintly.

"Please, sir."

"Who are you?"

It was then I noticed that the child's garment was wet through. He spoke more slowly now, as if the very life of him was ebbing away.

"Flee, sir." Yes, that was what he was saying. It was a warning. "Flee..." And, as if he were a dream, a nightmare vision, the child was no longer there.

I was deathly tired. Up the stairs. The bedroom. Lock the door. Out of my clothes. The relief of those warm, welcoming sheets. Sleep.

And, yes, a certain comfort. As usual, I was

half-woken by the cat alighting on my stomach. I sighed.

But it was not the sound of my own breath I heard. Like the whispering of the wind through the trees outside, it was the voice of a child.

Flee, sir.

I opened my eyes to look down on the shape that was lying on me.

"My lord."

When it looked up, what I had thought was a cat had the face of a woman, her smiling mouth smeared with blood, her hair clogged and matted. My chest, upon which she rested, was bare. Beside my heart were two neat wounds.

"Margaret, why?" I said, feeling no fear now, only an unbearable sense of loss, of betrayal. "Why?"

And my voice became a long, peaceful sigh as I felt myself falling into a swoon of silence, and down, down into the sweetest and deepest of sleeps.

I am a man of fact and I have tried to record, as factually as I am able, the extraordinary "paranormal" fantasy that the combination of my research and a nasty bout of flu inflicted upon me. I am only grateful that my natural common sense has allowed me to put the weird mental aberrations caused by a temporary fever in their proper context.

Today, on this Christmas morning, I am well again. Mr Forder's mission to "rescue" me has been cancelled. By the turn of the year, I fully expect to have delivered the final fatal stake to the heart of the vampire myth.

Gilbert and Maggie (a new friend, despite being the creature of my weirdest fantasy) now eat with me of an evening. Indeed the meals that Gilbert prepares are of such magnificence that I find I am dramatically gaining weight – to the extent that, as I write, my body tugs at the buttons of my shirt and the very hand with which I write this report seems to swell before my eyes.

I fear that a diet may be ordained when I return home to resume my career, writing books and visiting schools. I can hardly wait to tell my young audiences about the triumph of fact at Oxburgh Hall.

Gather round, children, I shall say. *This morning I shall explain to you why there is no such thing as a vampire.*

Mummy! Mummy!

K. M. Peyton

The school's Christmas treat was a visit to Lord Highmoor's Museum of Egyptian Treasures.

"Oh yuck, that's all I need for Christmas," moaned Craig Whitaker to his friend Harry. "A new bike is what I want, not a visit to a mummy."

"I'm getting a new bike," said Darren Porter, who already had everything. His old one was a gorgeous racer. Darren Porter had new bikes every year, like other people had socks.

"I'll have your cast-off," Craig said eagerly. "You won't be needing it if you're getting a new one."

"You'll be lucky!"

Craig knew he hadn't much to look forward to, the way his family was fixed, but it was a bit sickening to know that Darren's desirable old bike was going to waste away in the back of a garage when it could have a whole new life with him.

No point worrying though. Life was like that.

It was snowing – although more sleet than snow – when they trailed in an untidy crocodile after old Splodger, their teacher, across the town square and up the steps of the forbidding museum building. Splodger lost no time.

"Mummies," he proclaimed as they entered the museum, "are real bodies preserved by embalming in a special way. The word 'mummy' comes from the word 'mumia' which means bitumen, because the end result sometimes looked as if the body was covered in bitumen. But it wasn't. See here."

Having climbed a long stone staircase into a severe, high-ceilinged room, he stopped his class in front of a glass case containing a body-shaped effigy, wrapped completely in faded brown linen bandages.

"Inside there is a real body." (He nearly said "a real live body" in his earnestness but saw the gaffe just in time.) "It says on the card here that it is the body of a fifteen-year-old boy called Mehetmet who lived two thousand years before Christ. That is four thousand years ago," he added, for those not very good at maths. "Yet if you were to unwrap those bandages you would see him just as he was, four thousand years ago. A bit dried up perhaps," he thought he should add.

"I shall explain how they did it. When this boy died, he was laid on a slab and washed with salt water. Then his side was slit open and his entrails were pulled out, also his lungs, his stomach and his liver. Rather as your mother might buy a chicken and gut it."

He was rather old and hadn't caught up with the fact that all their mothers bought chickens from Tesco that were wrapped in plastic and looked as if they had never had guts.

"They always left the heart in. Then they stuffed the cavities with moss and sand and herbs and grass and things, so that they filled the skin out again. And then they took the brains out by inserting a rod up the left nostril and pulling it all out with a hook."

At this point two feeble girls had to go to the loo.

Craig Whitaker thought, *Poor old Mehetmet.* But he hadn't been old, after all, only six years older than himself, probably captain of Egyptian football. (Craig knew that football was a very ancient game, played in ancient times with a pig's bladder.)

"After that the body was soaked in a salt called natron for forty days, then dried off, covered with resin, and finally wrapped in linen bandages. The end result is that inside there is a perfectly preserved body."

The whole class breathed heavily in silence for some moments, staring at the bundle laid out before them.

"Why did they go to all that trouble?" asked a cool, intelligent girl called Selena. "We just burn ours, or bury them, no trouble at all."

"Because they believed that when they died they needed their bodies in an afterlife. The mummified bodies were put in boxes – there are some over there – beautifully painted with a likeness of the person all covered in decorations. And in the tomb they put useful things that the person might need, cooking gear and suchlike, even loaves of bread and bags of corn, and models of servants and animals, and a model of a boat with oars, all very practical. Even the poorest people were roughly embalmed before being put away. Mostly the mummies that were brought back from Egypt by collectors were those of very rich people whose tombs were very grand and full of treasures."

"Collectors? Thieves more like," said Darren in his sneery way.

"Hark who's talking," whispered Craig to Harry. Darren's father, a car dealer, was of great interest to the local police. Harry's father was a policeman so Harry knew these things.

"Yes, Darren, certainly the Victorian gentlemen plundered many treasures from abroad, but remember they were usually helped by the locals who were paid for their trouble. The locals had little regard for the stuff. It would be quite different today, of course."

His class, Splodger was gratified to see, was very taken with the mummies, and spent some time staring at Mehetmet as if willing him to open up and show them his remains. The mummy lay on his back, very straight, with his arms laid across his chest, the fingers pointing up towards his face. Each finger was meticulously, separately bandaged. There was a glass case over the mummy and a red rope round it to keep people off.

Craig and Harry stared at the drawing that an artist had made of a "reconstruction" of Mehetmet's face.

"It says they can tell, from scanning through the bandages, what he looked like. He's still all there, inside."

Craig felt a bit funny. Mehetmet in the reconstruction was looking at him in a curious way, as if it was he, Craig, who was the exhibit. He had a bit of a smile and looked friendly. A bit joky. He was inside the bandages, just as he once had been, looking joky. He looked like he would play tricks. Craig thought he could sense him, pleased to have a load of visitors much his own age, instead of old ladies. He would like to get up and join them, and go out in the town, on a bus perhaps. He only knew about sand and deserts and the pyramids and suchlike. He would find their place quite an eye-opener, all cars and shoppers and the Salvation Army bawling out carols round the Christmas tree outside. How strange! Fancy him ending up in this old museum!

"I like him," Craig whispered to Harry.

But when he looked up and took in the large decorated coffins and painted mummy covers that filled the gloomy room, he felt his spirits sink. The presence of death bore in, if you looked around. The walls were covered with knives and spears and instruments of death. What an awful place to end up in!

"Creepy, ennit?" he muttered to Harry.

Darren came muscling in, scornful as usual. "Frightened of a few old corpses?" he sneered.

"Who said I was frightened? I just said creepy."

"Bet you'd be scared stiff in here alone, at night!"

"Bet I wouldn't!"

"Go on, prove it! I bet – I bet you wouldn't dare stay in this room all night, when everyone's gone."

"Bet me what? Bet I would! I wouldn't be frightened."

"Garn, you'd die of the shivers," said Darren.

"Bet me then!" Craig saw his chance and

pounced. "Your old bike – you bet me your old bike I'll stay in here all night?"

"You'd do it for my old bike? Done!" Darren's eyes glittered. "You gotta be locked in, right, when the old geezers shut up shop. I'll be watching, make sure you don't slip out. That's a deal. And I'll be here when it opens, see you go through with it."

"Hey, come off it. How can you?" Harry said. "They turf everyone out at five o'clock."

"Go on! The old geezer only glances in when the time comes. You could easily get in one of these boxes, put your head down. He wouldn't see you."

Darren gestured to one of the big decorated boxes that used to hold the mummy's coffin and all the accoutrements that went in the tomb. Unlike the mummy, it wasn't in a glass case, but just had the red rope round it.

Craig considered. Yes, it could be done. The worst that could happen would be that they were seen and pitched out. No problem.

"Harry can come too. The two of us."

Darren agreed, after a bit of humming and hawing. "No cheating. I'll make sure we have witnesses that you don't come out at closing time, only in the morning."

"It doesn't open till ten. We'll do it on Friday night," Craig decided.

Darren sniggered. "I'll have an ambulance

standing by. Take you to the nuthouse."

He strolled on after Splodger and the rest of the class, leaving Craig and Harry contemplating the coffin box.

"Bit of a squash," said Harry. "And thank you very much for inviting me. Cheers. Who gets the bike?"

"I'll let you ride it," Craig offered with a grin.

Craig found his pulse rate had gone up, looking round the depressing room he was to spend the night in. There were no windows, only skylights. The ceiling was high, the walls covered mostly with killing instruments. Glittering blades looked nasty even in daylight. There were four other mummies besides Mehetmet and several jars said to contain the removed entrails, stomach, etc. Yuck! The coffin box was just big enough to take them both with a squash. The lid was open, propped with a stick, so that the visitors could see the decorations within. The floor of the box carried a map to help the dead person's soul find its way (where to?) and had eyes painted on the sides so that he "could see the sunrise". There was also a door in the side for the spirit to fly out of.

"Weird, eh?" Harry murmured, as they browsed around. The room had taken on a completely new significance since the conversation with Darren.

"It's a doddle," Craig said.

He was so excited about getting the bike that he was determined to convince himself that the idea really was a doddle. But he knew perfectly well that he had an active imagination and could get frightened in the dark without any encouragement from the odd mummy. He tried not to think what lay ahead, to think only about the bike.

They told their mothers they were staying the night with each other, and Darren himself accompanied them to the museum shortly before closing time on Friday night.

"When they ring the closing bell I'll chat up the gaffer and then if he asks where you are I'll say you went out ahead of me."

Darren had his pal Skinner with him, another rat like himself. They carried bulging school bags like Craig and Harry, who had filled theirs with provisions to get through the night. Mars bars and things.

"Like old Mehetmet," Harry said.

Darren said they had sports gear. They were going to the leisure centre.

"We'll think of you while we're enjoying ourselves. See you come out in the morning, or no deal. No bike."

They went in twenty minues or so before closing time, warned by the gaffer in the hall that they didn't have long. Craig noticed Darren talking to one of the other attendants, a spotty youth, in the hall downstairs on their way out, and wondered if he was telling him what was up. The youth was obviously a friend of his, for they were laughing together. The old boy upstairs was looking at his watch, yawning. They hadn't even started yet, and Craig found he was sweating with fright. He assured himself it was just the initial hassle that was frightening him, avoiding the old boy when the bell rang for closing. He stood by Harry, staring at a gruesome painting of the British army getting speared by Zulus in the Boer war. Plenty of spilt entrails here, and not tidily put away in pots either. Even Harry turned away, looking pale. Darren and Skinner were giggling away in the same room. Craig and Harry drifted into the mummy room. Harry looked as sick as Craig felt.

"It'll be OK when they've all gone," Craig said. "We'll get used to it then."

When the lights go out, Harry thought. He shivered.

The closing bell rang. Craig and Harry could hear Darren chatting to the old boy next door.

"Come on."

They crossed over to the coffin box and, taking care not to knock against the stick that held the lid up, they climbed into the box, pulling their kit in after them. It was a squash, but not terrible. They lay down, wriggling silently into position, scarcely breathing. The only sound was the pulsing of their own hearts. Craig felt the sweat of fear running down his back – and they hadn't even started yet.

"All out! Out, you boys!" came the voice of the old boy, but not close. He was in the doorway between the two rooms.

"I thought your pals were in here?" they heard him say.

"No, they went straight out. They didn't stay in here," Darren lied nonchalantly. He was a great liar, could look you in the eye without a blink. Craig heard the man's footsteps coming towards them and thought they were sussed, but no, he went on past. The man couldn't have cast a glance in their direction, otherwise he was bound to see them.

He shouted, "Come on, you two, I want my tea."

"Just popping in the loo, mate," said Darren.

"Not so much of the mate. Be sharp then."

The footsteps all went away and the boys heard them echoing down the stairs to the hall below. Harry sat up.

"That's done it then."

Had he been hoping to be discovered? Craig knew he had half wanted it. Now there was complete silence and all the lights had gone out, he didn't feel any less frightened than before. More, if anything. And there was all night to go yet! Ghosts didn't get up at tea-time, for heaven's sake! The town hall clock was striking five.

But Harry sat up against the end of the box, making himself comfortable, and rummaged in his bag for provisions. He pulled out a bottle of Coke and some doughnuts. Craig watched him dubiously. They were sitting in the coffin, he wanted to point out. But it was, admittedly, quite cosy and comfortable.

"Just make sure that stick thing is well stuck in, to keep the lid up."

Harry examined it. "Yes, it's in slots. It's OK."

It was December and dark outside, but the bright lights of the town cast an orange glow through the skylights, so it wasn't pitch dark in the room. Dark enough though. A muffled roar of commuter traffic comforted, but that would soon go. Usually the town centre was dead at night. Not even vandals and yobbos found it worth plundering as a rule. But now it was nearly Christmas it was busier, and the town hall was playing carols which came and went on gusts of wind.

Harry said, "I wouldn't put it past Darren to trick the old boy and come back in here, stay the night as well. Make noises to put the wind up us. You know. It's the sort of thing he'd like."

"You think? Going to the loo – might have been

a trick, yeah. And he had plenty of gear with him."

Craig wasn't sure if he found this comforting or not. He was already as jumpy as a cat. Harry's doughnut stuck in this throat. He could see Mehetmet lying there, only a couple of metres away: a real body. *Don't think about it!*

"Yeah, well, if we hear any funny business out there, I reckon it'll be those sickos."

They had brought torches to read by but the supply of comics soon ran out and without their computer games the time hung heavily. The rush hour faded and the town outside wound up its carols and fell silent, save for the hours passing on its clock. A moon came up and competed with the sodium glow, giving an eerie light inside the mummy room, throwing long shadows across the floor. The upright mummy cases seemed to stand taller and taller. The knives on the wall glittered.

Harry reckoned it would be best to go to sleep. He had gone rather quieter now, Craig noticed. If there were ghosts, ghost time was approaching. The half-hour before midnight struck.

"Let's get comfortable," Harry said.

Lying with a head up each end, feet in the middle, there was room. The central heating was still on, although it was much cooler, so they needed their anoraks on. They'd thought to bring a cushion each for a pillow – sleeping bags would have been nice, but too bulky to bring in.

"Not bad at all," Harry conceded.

They lay pretending to sleep. The town hall clock struck midnight. Craig lay rigid, staring up. The moon glared back at him, picking out the decorations all down the side of the box and the drawing of the little door where the spirit departed. Mehetmet's spirit. The body that lay there beside them, almost within touching distance. A body! It was the closest Craig had ever been to a body. Bodies were tucked away safely these days in funeral homes, out of sight, not left out in the parlour to look at as in days of yore. You didn't meet a body any more. But here he was, spending the night with a body, and the night was long. *Don't think about it. Think about the bike, Harry Potter, anything. Shut your eyes.* Was it his imagination, or were there sighs and rustlings in the room? He opened his eyes. The moonlight shining on a curved sabre on the wall missed its tip which was in shadow, and the darkness there looked like the blood which had once undoubtedly stained it. Craig could hear the drip of it. Drip, drip, drip. He sat up. Yes, there was definitely a noise. Dripping. The entrails slithering out of the dead body...

He sat up.

"Harry!"

"What!"

"What's that dripping noise?"

Harry listened.

"The central heating," he said.

Craig didn't believe him. Harry didn't sound convinced. But it wasn't much use arguing. The dripping seemed to fade, but soon another noise took over, a scuttering. Hesitant. Scutter, scutter scutter, then silence. Craig, trying not to, lifted his head and looked over the side of the box. In the moonlight he saw a big rat scuttling along the wall.

He tried not to scream, not entirely successfully.

"What's up?" Harry squeaked.

"A rat!"

Harry looked out.

"You're joking!"

"No, I saw it! Running along the wall."

"Feeding off those goodies in the jars," Harry said and laughed.

Craig felt sick, but Harry's common sense calmed him. He felt a fool and a coward, and determined to do better. Go to sleep. Keep the mind off bodies and think of Newcastle United. He shut his eyes firmly.

He dozed off at last. He slept.

Cramp woke him. His right leg was agony. He shifted, not knowing where he was, and the pain shafted through his calf. What a hard bed! He opened his eyes and could see nothing. Total darkness. He shut his eyes, opened them again, and it made no difference. Where was he?

Then, kicking Harry, he remembered. The coffin, the museum! But where was the moonlight, where the glittering knives, the towering coffin cases? He put out a hand and felt the wooden wall of the coffin case hard against him. But why the pitch darkness? Even if the moon had gone, the town lights had filled the windows.

Craig sat up and banged his head hard. The shock made him squeal, brought his brain to life. He couldn't see a thing because the coffin lid was down! Impossible!

"Harry!"

He pushed against the lid to no avail.

"Harry!"

Jeez, they were shut in the coffin!

"Harry!" This time he shouted, screamed.

Harry jumped up and crashed his head.

"Yow! What the –?"

"The lid's come down!"

"What lid?"

Harry was still half asleep. "Where am I? What – hey, I can't see a thing!"

"We're in the coffin, idiot, and the lid's come down. Did you knock it?"

"No, of course not. That stick was lodged in – there was a special hole for it. It can't have come down!"

Their muffled voices were shrill with panic. Craig felt sweating hot, suffocating. Suppose the air couldn't get in and they died of suffocation! He remembered a terrible story he had once read, about a girl who hid in a chest during a game of hide and seek, and the lid came down, the latch clicked to ... her skeleton was found years later.

But no, the museum would open in the morning...

Harry said, "I told you, Darren stayed in to scare us. He's let it down!"

Craig felt a great wave of relief flood over him. Of course!

"Yes, that's it! It couldn't have come down by itself."

"Saying he was going to the loo – I think he's mates with that younger attendant. They were laughing together. I bet he worked it all out."

Soon he would come to see how scared they were.

"Well, now we know it's him, it's not scary at all," Craig said bravely.

Actually, even if it was Darren, it was scary as hell. Being in such darkness, and knowing it was a coffin, wasn't comforting for all the fine words that came out of his mouth. Darren must have done it. There was no way it could have happened otherwise. It was terribly stuffy in the box, and now they knew they couldn't get out they suddenly had cramp all over and wriggled and twisted to relieve their pains.

Craig remembered the little door for the spirit to fly out of, and groped around until he found the hinge. He fiddled with it and pushed, and a tiny square of light appeared as he managed to open it. Now at least they wouldn't suffocate. Then he remembered the rat and thought that perhaps the rat would jump in. The thought of being shut in the coffin with a rat scrabbling over him made him come out in another great sweat of horror. He would *rather* suffocate! He pulled the little door to. He didn't want to lose his soul either, come to that, if it were thinking of escaping. What a situation they were in! It was very hard to stay cool, even with the thought of Darren's bike. The utter darkness was unnerving, something he had never experienced before. And being so uncomfortable, it was hard not to give in to the temptation to kick out and fight and swear and let the panic take over. But that wouldn't help things. All the same, the feeling of claustrophobia threatened to undo him. He could hear Harry making a whimpering noise and felt like joining in.

"It's horrible!"

"It's only Darren playing tricks." He tried to make his voice soothing and calm.

Whatever to do? The thought of being stuck there for another eight hours or so was horrifying.

"If we both push against it as hard as we can, perhaps we can get it open."

"We'll break it!"

"So what? We can't stay like this."

"Darren'll come, surely?"

"Well, I'm not waiting."

With the threat of panic perilously close to overtaking him, Craig turned himself over and thrust against the lid with his back as hard as he could. Harry got the idea and did the the same. Nothing happened. It was like attacking rock. They tried and tried. Now the panic was rising fast.

Craig sobbed out curses against Darren. He must be able to hear their crashings around in the box! How he must be laughing!

"One more try!" he shouted to Harry. "One, two, three..."

With which the lid opened without so much as a faint splintering of wood, without any resistance at all!

In the sudden light they faced each other, kneeling up, feeling unutterably relieved. And very stupid.

"Darren!" they shouted.

Their voices echoed, sounding like laughter, round the great silent room. The call came back from the adjoining rooms like the sound of a foreign bird from distant forests. It was so weird they could not bring themselves to call again. They climbed out of the box and tried to forget how frightened they had been.

"It's OK now. We can sleep on the floor. I'm not getting back in there again," Harry said.

"Nor me," said Craig fervently. Rat or no rat. It was Darren who was the rat. "I'll see if I can find him, show him his trick didn't work."

That was bluster and he knew it for Darren had frightened them nearly to death. But everything was OK now. The big echoing room was positively friendly after the horrors of the coffin. He walked through the adjoining rooms but there was no sign of Darren. Probably he was hiding in the loos downstairs. But, for all his relief, Craig didn't feel like exploring alone amongst this exhibition of grisly deeds from the past. He went back, rather subdued, to where Harry was trying to make himself comfortable with his lone cushion on the floor. He had closed the lid of the coffin.

"I can't find that stick thing that was keeping it up. Darren must have taken it."

"It doesn't matter."

"What's the time?"

"Three o'clock."

As he settled down to try and get back to sleep Craig wondered whether the bike was going to be worth it. He had never felt so frightened in his life before. But he wouldn't let on to Darren ... it was weird to find out what real terror felt like. It made him sweat just to think of it. He lay down next to Harry, getting comfortable on his side, and found himself staring straight at Mehetmet's corpse. He looked up at the drawing of the joky face, and was in such a confused state that he was sure one eye winked at him. He sat up, gibbering.

"I can't stay here!"

He moved across the floor, remembered the rat, and came back beside Harry. Harry was already asleep again. The boy had no imagination. Craig lay down, facing firmly away from Mehetmet. He heard the town hall clock strike the half-hour, then four, the half-hour again. The floor grew harder and harder. No doubt Darren knew a way out and was home in bed now, waiting to laugh at them when they emerged at ten o'clock.

He slept.

When he awoke it was light. Eight o'clock! The traffic was flowing with cheerful noise outside, the carols were blasting out again, the sun was shining in through the skylights and Mehetmet looked just like what he was, a bundle of dried-up old rag and bones. Craig stared at him. Something was different. What was it? Craig propped himself up on one elbow, feeling his heart thumping unsteadily, his throat taut with a feeling of sickness. Mehemet's bandaged fingers, which had lain so tidily on his chest, palms down, now stuck up vertically, pressed together as if in prayer. Quite still. Craig felt himself trembling, more frightened now than ever Darren could have hoped for.

Harry was still asleep. The coffin's lid was propped up with its stick, just as it had been when they'd started the night.

Craig stared at it. It had been closed when he went to sleep. What on earth was going on? He shook Harry awake.

"You see Darren in the night?" His voice came out like a mouse's squeak. He cleared his throat sternly. "The lid's propped up again with the stick. He must have come back."

But even Darren couldn't have rearranged the fingers. The mummy was still in its glass case. Craig couldn't bring himself to mention the hands. His memory must be playing him tricks. The hands must have been like that all along and he had just remembered it wrong.

"I never saw him," Harry said.

Craig took great pains to steady his voice. "I suppose he wanted to leave things as they should be, else we'd get into trouble. If we're caught getting out, that is."

"Where the hell is he hiding? Let's have a look for him."

They got up to go looking, and Craig made himself ignore the beckoning Mehetmet. He felt Mehetmet was having him on, a joky boy. But Mehetmet had died four thousand years ago!

They searched every room, the coffee shop and the toilets, but there was no sign of anybody. There was a window in the toilets that let out into a back street, but it was locked.

"I reckon he had the key from that mate of his, and got in and out here," Harry said. "It wouldn't be difficult. He'll be home eating his breakfast by now."

Harry was starving, but the coffee shop was cleaned bare of cake and biscuits, the cupboards locked. Craig pretended that he was dying for something to eat, but knew that he would be incapable of digesting a crumb. They went back into the mummy room and he went to the glass case. Mehetmet's hands were palm-down on his chest, just as they had been at the beginning. Craig stared, not knowing who was playing tricks on whom. Was his memory so uncertain? It wasn't possible! As he hadn't mentioned the changing of the hands to Harry he said nothing now, but just stood staring, praying for an explanation. But explanation came there none. There wasn't one! He looked at the reconstructed drawing. That joky face. Did one eye wink? He blinked, looked again. The face stared back.

"Come on," Harry was saying. "They'll be opening soon. We'll have to hide up somewhere. Not in the coffin again! We can just sit behind it."

Craig looked at the coffin. It stood there with the lid up, just as it had been the evening before. Everything was perfect, just as it should be, Mehetmet's hands in their proper place, no sign of disturbance anywhere.

Harry was convinced that Darren had been shut in, too, and shut the coffin lid down. Craig supposed that might be part of the explanation but he was so tired and confused that he could no longer think straight. Nervous, too, about getting into trouble if the attendants found them.

"Well, they can't do anything," Harry said. "We haven't done any damage, we left everything as it was."

The town hall clock struck ten at last. They ducked down to hide (but not in the coffin!) hoping to slip out unseen, with perhaps Darren to make a diversion. They heard the keepers arrive downstairs and the ticket lady setting up her stall. The voices echoed through the empty rooms.

"If we wait till some visitors arrive, it'll be easier."

Luckily a large clutch of French students came in, making a good racket, asking questions, and they were able to scurry down the stairs and out through the entrance before the ticket lady could ask any questions. She gaped after them, but by then they were turning up their faces into the gorgeous winter sunshine and trying hard not to cheer out loud.

Darren and Skinner were sitting on the wall outside.

"So, how was it?"

"A doddle, except for your stupid tricks," shouted Harry. "How did you get in and out so easily? Through that mate of yours, I suppose?"

"What are you talking about?"

"That trick you pulled, shutting us in the coffin."

Darren stared. "Hey, it's got to you. Shutting you in what coffin? We weren't there, you prat. It was your night alone, remember? We never volunteered to spend it with you."

"You must have been! How else…" Craig's voice quivered. There had to be an answer! But Darren was quite obviously not putting it on.

"We told you, we went down the leisure centre.

Then we had fish and chips – quite late by then – got home and went to bed. Ask our *mummies*!"

"We just got up and came here. Haven't even had breakfast yet," Skinner added.

"We thought you'd come out raving mad. Seems like you have. What did the ghostie do to you then, diddums?"

Darren was back to his sneery ways again. It seemed quite obvious to Craig that he was telling the truth. There was no hidden glee, no teasing, no sense of having triumphed, only a rather bored and glum acceptance of the fact that he had lost his bike.

"You can collect it at lunchtime," he said. "See you then."

The two of them sauntered off.

Craig felt sick. Later they asked around and found out it was true that Darren and Skinner had been around the town all night. The loo window, they discovered, was rusted up and hadn't been opened for years. There was no way they could have been in the museum too.

"Maybe we just dreamt it," Harry said.

"Mehetmet did it."

The more he thought about it, the more Craig was convinced that that was the truth. There was no other explanation. Harry never said any more, and neither of them ever spoke about their experience again. It was too uncomfortable to think about.

And, strangely enough, Craig never enjoyed riding the bike he had coveted so much. Every time he rode it and his hands were on the handlebars he kept seeing them wrapped in tiny bandages, resting on the grips. He took to wearing heavy gloves every time he rode, but it made no difference. Those beautiful bandaged fingers were always before his eyes, making fun of him.

He passed the bike on to his younger brother in a couple of months' time, and took to skate-boarding instead.

Babushka

Tony Mitton

Babushka was a busy woman,
never, ever still,
washing, dusting, sweeping round
each step, each ledge, each sill.
No speck of dust lay on her floor,
no cobweb laced her pane.
But when Babushka finished
it was time to start again.

So when a new star shone up high,
she took no special heed.
The pathway needed sweeping,
there were vegetables to weed.
But as she knelt and worked away
three men came riding by.
They paused beside her cottage
to view the evening sky.

They wore the dust of many days,
of travel slow and far.
But now they gazed in wonder
at the newly shining star.
Babushka stood and greeted them,
"Good sirs, you're tired, I see.
So be my guests. I offer you
my hospitality."

They graciously accepted.
Babushka took them in.
They marvelled how her cottage shone,
so welcoming within.
And as Babushka bustled
to bring them cheer and rest,
they told her of their journey,
their strange and sacred quest.

"We go to pay our tribute
to a great and glorious king,
with gold and frankincense and myrrh,
these presents that we bring.
The star above will lead us
to this Saviour of the Earth,
as all creation celebrates
the moment of his birth."

Then suddenly Babushka
was seen to slow and pause,
as if she'd lost the purpose
of her endless, restless chores.
"A child," she murmured sadly.
"Just like my own dear boy,
who died and took away with him
my passion and my joy."

"But children make a mess," she frowned.
"They fill one's life with care."
And once again Babushka started
bustling everywhere.
The three men smiled quietly
and one began to say,
"Come with us, dear Babushka,
and join us on our way."

"What, leave my chores and tasks?" she cried.
"To go along with you?
I simply cannot. No!" she said.
"There's far too much to do!"
And as she tidied round them,
she shook her busy head.
So soon the weary travellers
went tiredly to bed.

But in the dawn they pressed once more,
"Babushka, think again.
To see the Holy Saviour child
might ease your grief and pain."
Babushka paused, then thought aloud,
"I have a plan in mind...
But do not wait. Make speed," she said.
"I'll follow on behind."

So, as the three men rode away,
Babushka went inside.
She opened up a cupboard door,
and as she looked, she cried.
For on the shelves were many toys
belonging to her boy.
She meant to patch and mend them
for this new child to enjoy.

When all the toys were ready
the day was growing late.
Babushka took them in a sack
and latched her little gate.
And as she met with passers-by
she asked them of the men.
She took the way they pointed out,
time and time again.

And after several days had passed
she came upon an inn.
"A child was born," the landlord said,
"to save the world from sin.
But soldiers came to kill him,
so the family fled away.
And where you'll find them now," he frowned,
"there's nobody can say."

So off Babushka went again,
her toys inside her sack.
She wandered through the gentle plain.
She took the mountain track.
She journeyed through the seasons.
She plodded through the years.
She passed the people on her way,
their smiles, their frowns, their tears.

Till one day, many years from then,
she stopped and deeply sighed.
For on a hill there hung a man,
so cruelly crucified.
His face was all compassion,
though they'd nailed him to a cross.
And at his feet his mother grieved,
lamenting for her loss.

Babushka stopped to comfort her,
"I lost my son, like you.
There is no grief like mother's loss,
and nothing you can do,
except to go on living
through wind and sun and rain,
and hope that all the weathers
slowly wash away the pain."

Babushka did not know the man
for the child she'd searched to find.
Half-ghost, half-human now she seemed,
and wandering in her mind.
But from that day her burden
weighed lighter on her back.
And if she chanced on children,
she'd dip into her sack.

"All children come to save us,"
she'd smile and sadly say,
then leave them little presents
and quietly walk away.
And though she gave so freely,
by some strange miracle,
across the years her sack of toys
stayed always stacked up full.

And even now, past cottages
and farms by snowy woods,
Babushka shoulders patiently
her sack of precious goods.
And when the country children
find her gifts, they smile and say,
"Babushka's been. She's left a toy.
Hurrah for Christmas Day!"

The Ghost of Christmas Shopping

Lesley Howarth

I'm a ghost, right? Haunting's my job. I get up and around, most years, about December the twenty-third. Or maybe the twenty-fourth. Call me lazy, but I never went much on getting up before I had to. There was a time, back when it's hard to remember, when I spent my life in bed. In hospital, that was. Then I got so I was OK to go home. Then I could go out shopping, so long as I didn't overdo it, or carry anything heavy. I left carrying things to Mum. I had to be careful a lot. I'm careful now. Catch me getting out of the freezer much before December the twenty-third, and you've got an exceptionally fine Christmas shopping frenzy.

I usually start flexing the old haunting muscles about the time most kids finally realize the chocolate in the advent calendar's the grisliest ever invented. Once the shoppers in the supermarket get that glazed look, when they'll buy just about anything with "Festive Special" on it, that's about the time I stretch my legs. When they open up the freezer for those last-minute cocktail-size sausage rolls, that's my wake-up call. It's shopping fever that warms me up and sets me on my feet. Call me shallow, but I love that stuff. I suppose you could call me the ghost of Christmas shopping, except no one calls me anything. Ever. I did have another name, once.

Usually, I wake up in the frozen turkeys. Then I huff out when someone opens the freezer – you can have enough of frozen turkeys, know what I mean? Soon as I'm out of the freezer, I'm checking out trolleys for a likely family to hang out with over Christmas. A really classic trolley always grabs me.

So this year I'm cruising the aisles, right, and the trolleys are looking pretty mediocre, nothing too appealing – when I actually spot the Stantons. I almost die, except I did that already. See, I almost made it to lunchtime, last Christmas Day with the Stantons. Except for Danny Stanton's puppy, I might be there now. The stuff with the puppy almost killed me all over again. *Look at him, isn't he great? What'll I call him? Rusty? Come on, Rusty. Thanks, Mum, thanks, Dad. I really, really love him.*

Phew. Too much of that stuff, and I'm gone. Back in the freezer till next year. Love, generosity, Christmas spirit – it really turns me off. Call me freezer-fungus, just don't give me any of that heart-warming stuff. Maybe I am freezer-fungus, but I have to have something to feed off, you know? Even mould needs something to work with. I have to have hurt feelings, or at least a bit of rage. But Christmas spirit gets me. It makes me throw, it really does. I have to go back to my freezer. I don't have a lot of choice. It was too much to hope I'd make it through with the Stantons. Far too selfless, the Stantons. Pretty bleak Christmas all round.

So I've never yet made a whole Christmas Day with anyone. So I'm thinking this year could be a first, and I'm chilling out on the corner between the deli and the Country Baker mince pie offer, when I spot the perfect trolley. Very low fruit content, triple-choc super-soft ice-cream plus soft drinks so bright they bring on an additive high just looking at them. This is a trolley I can relate to. I tag along after the family. Mum, Dad, boy, girl. The little girl could be a problem. The little girl sees straight through me, and I know she's got me sussed.

"Kelly," Mum asks her, "wake up. What colour jelly d'you fancy?"

"Blackcurrant," goes Kelly, staring hard. "Tell him to go away."

"Who?" says Mum, "Lawrie?"

It looks like Lawrie's the brother. He's not much older than Kelly. He could be younger than Kelly, who knows? What am I, expert on children?

"Not Lawrie." Old Kelly's going to blow it in a minute. I dredge up a smile, but she pulls Mum's coat and points. "Not Lawrie," she says, "that boy. Why's he following us?"

Mum looks round. "What boy? Lawrie, get me a cheesecake mix? Down a bit. Left a bit. There."

"Go away!" Kelly pouts. "I don't like that boy."

Phew. I make a face. It doesn't matter what I do. Mum's not really listening.

"Push the trolley," says Mum, "good girl. Let's get some biscuits, shall we? How about one of those selection tins with the pink wafers in it, would you like that?"

Lawrie drops a packet of cheesecake mix into the trolley. "I want one of those chocolate things," he says.

Lawrie points and he's right. I have to admit, the Festive Yule Log offer's pretty tempting. Lawrie's mother agrees.

"We'll have a Yule Log as well," she says. "And some frozen eclairs."

Top shoppers, or what? I'm warming to this lot already. Dad wanders off to the Wines and Spirits. I trail the others round the freezers. They're real

117

shopaholics, I'm glad to say. By the time we reach the checkout the trolley's landsliding twelve-pack crisps, ham, mallows, jelly, Father-Christmas-shaped novelty bars, oven chips, party-poppers, crackers, Bumper Nut Assortments, Country Baker mince pies, ready-to-roll icing, instant trifle mix, cake, pudding, mini-rolls, Festive Flavour Corn Puffs, Yule Log, sausage rolls, plus two fat selection stockings. And that's just the stuff on top. Gross-out, or what? This is the family of my dreams.

I always did eat a lot. When I wasn't a ghost, I was fourteen. Then it was crisps, chips, biscuits, burgers, anything junky, OK? Now I'm a ghost, I feed on that special Christmas feeling of never having enough of whatever it was you really wanted. So you open all your presents, and the CD you got isn't right. The sweater someone bought you is almost right, except for the colour, are they blind? Plus your family's driving you mad. You wonder what Christmas is for, until Pictionary or Twister after dinner. Then the arguments start, and every other Christmas you ever remember comes flooding back with a bad taste, and instead of feeling sorry you feel spoilt and fed-up and ungrateful, like Christmas never gives you what you think it will, and somehow there must be more. That's what keeps me going. I always wanted more. Except every year, someone blows it. Sooner or later, someone does something nice or generous or heartwarming, and I'm gone. Can't stick that kind of thing.

Trolleys can tell you a lot. With a top trolley, no dates in sight – never bother haunting anyone with dates in their trolley, only sad people who never argue buy dates – the Bayleys make my day. I know they're called the Bayleys because I check out the cheque at the checkout. The squabble over the prawn crisps clinches it. The Battling Bayleys. I can feel it. I'm going to have a really joyful Christmas.

Kelly stuffs crisps and stares at me while her folks load up the car. You can get kids like this sometimes, the kind that's going to spot you right away. They tend to be a pain, except it doesn't matter too much what they say if they're little, because no one's going to believe they saw a ghost. Kelly's little. Six, maybe seven. I reckon it's a chance worth taking. I look back at the supermarket before we leave. Ta-ra. Bye for now. I've tried other stores, but you don't get the rush. Food shopping under pressure brings out the worst in people. I always come back to SuperFare.

OK, Christmas Eve with the Bayleys rates eight on the aggro scale. Enough bad vibes to snack off, not enough to pig out. I rove around the house for a while, sampling this room, then that. The kitchen tastes good to me. Mum unpacks the Christmas cake. She takes out the ready-rolled icing and gets it all stuck to her hands. Finally, she gets it on the cake. It looks like a badly-fitting nappy. She gets out the cake decorations and sticks on trees and a reindeer. The Father Christmas figure won't stand up. She screws him into the cake so he's up to his knees in Special Offer marzipan. She's getting pretty cross.

I'm enjoying myself quite a bit, when Dad throws a wobbler in the loft: "Where did that thingie with the brass cherubs on it go? You know. The thing you light candles on, and the cherubs go round and round? What? I'm not getting a thing about it. I'd just like to find it one year, that's all."

Dad comes downstairs and ruins his suede shoes dribbling hot UHT cream out of a Country Baker mince pie on to 'em. The kids watch a Christmas Eve ghost story on the telly. I have to tell you, the ghost in the story's pretty weak. If you're talking technique, I could show it a thing or two. Some ghosts go in for traditional stuff like busting mirrors, rapping on walls, turning lights and taps on and off, that kind of thing. Not me. I usually go for something simple but classy, like bending every clock hand in the house, crossing knives on the table, spelling out letters on the floor with whatever comes in handy, swapping keys around, etc., etc. Switch on the telly in the middle of the night and throw in a nightmare for the family dog, plus a pool of tomato ketchup on the settee, and you got 'em thoroughly spooked.

Anyway, Christmas Eve, around midnight, I slip into Kelly Bayley's room in reverse Father Christmas mode. Usually what I do is, I take all the kids' Christmas presents out of their sacks and distribute them in weird places. It always throws 'em on Christmas morning, when they wake up and find things upside down in the hall or undone all over the floor, and they realize nobody did it. It freaks 'em out every time. I've never known it fail.

Kelly's hit the jackpot this year. This year her Christmas sack's huge. Her parents have bought up every tacky plastic toy there is, plus they've left her two confectionery stockings. In front of everything else is Candy's House, Kelly's main present. I unwrap its pink-and-purple chimney. Candy's House is all pink-and-purple, and so is Candy's Stable and Candy's Styles, the hairdresser's shop with real shower-heads for real styles. I know these things, you see. I see them on TV. Kelly also has Poppy Pinhole, the Pocket-Sized Doll That's Your Friend. I stuff Poppy Pinhole down the chimney of Candy's House, and move on before I hurl.

Moving on down the sack, I take out a couple more presents. One of them feels like a game, the

121

other's a soft toy or something, so I drift out and leave it in the bath. I unwrap its head. It's a soft-toy Dalmatian puppy, cute or what? I leave it leering down the toilet with a shaving foam hat on its head. Then I drift into the kitchen and stick a few knives in the wall. It's not very nice, I know, but how else can I let them know I want less Christmas spirit, more aggro? Good thing the dog's in the garage. I know it knows I'm there.

So I shimmy back into the bedroom and ghost out a few more toys. It's quite exciting, you know? I makes me feel quite nostalgic. I had presents, once. Once I had a bike on Christmas morning. That was before I got ill. I think about what I was like before I got ill. Then I get out the Bumper Smarties from Kelly's Confectionery Stocking and spell out G - R - A - N - T in Smarties all over Kelly Bayley's bedroom floor, because Grant was my name when I had Christmases. I don't have Christmases now. Only the sparks off other people's. I could get sorry for myself.

To cheer myself up a bit, I put a few things in the fridge – a Bat-Ball, an Etch-a-Sketch and a pair of Glitter Leggings, and I hope they appreciate the joke. Back in the bedroom I spend quite a while balancing a board game over the door. Then just as I'm placing a Pocahontas Bubble Bath on the very edge of the bookcase, I hear a noise in the bed. I look around. She's watching me. Kelly Bayley's awake.

"Those aren't your presents," she says. "Father Christmas left them for me."

Ghosts never panic, OK? They can speak to you if they want to, it's just that most of them don't.

"Leave my presents alone," she says, "they're not for you, they're for me."

I know that – I'm just helping.

"No, you're not," she says, "you're hiding things, you are."

No, I'm not.

"You are."

I'm putting them in funny places.

"Well, you shouldn't. You should go home."

If only. Home, I think.

"You don't have a home, do you?" Kelly Bayley sits up and gives me the stare. "I know who you are," she says. "You're the supermarket ghost."

So? I send her, crushingly. What does she want, a medal?

"You needn't think –"

Needn't think what?

"You needn't think you're spoiling Christmas –"

Who's spoiling Christmas?

"– 'cos I won't let you." She rubs her eyes. She's tired. Good. With luck, I hope, in the morning, she won't remember a thing.

I never did nothing, all right? I only moved a few things.

"I can see what you're doing. It's mean."

It's only a joke, OK?

"Well, why don't you just stop doing it? Why don't you just go away?"

I don't usually get this kind of thing. It's pretty upsetting, actually. No one ever challenged me with those flashing brown eyes, the way Kelly Bayley does. With this kind of interference, the only thing to do is The Fade. I fade pretty quick, but is it ever a long time before she stops scouting the bedroom with those big brown eyes and finally goes back to sleep. By twelve forty-five I'm beginning to think the Bayleys may be my biggest mistake yet. I fade through the floor and rubbish the Christmas tree a bit, but it doesn't cheer me up as much as it usually does. For some reason.

'Tis the season to be jolly,
  Tra-la-la-la-la-la
  Tra-la-la—

Dad turns off the radio alarm. "Happy Christmas, love."

So it's Christmas morning and – BANG! – Kelly and Lawrie Bayley are in at their mum and dad's bedroom door and all over their mum and dad's bed with Christmas sacks and wrapping paper and tantrums, which is great, I mean, I'm in.

The first thing that happens is Lawrie stands on his remote-control car. It's only his main present. He doesn't mean to. He didn't see it. He only just unwrapped it, and now it's bro-oh-oh-ken!

"And whose fault is that?" Dad says.

Lawrie's wail climbs higher and higher, till Dad packs the car away and says he'll look at it later. He can look at it all he likes, it'll still be broken.

"It's broken an' you have to mend it!" Lawrie's spoilt tantrum explodes.

"I'll try to," Dad says. "Please."

"An' you get your tool-box please, an' you mend it now!"

"Lawrie," Dad says, "that will do."

"Please. Can you. Mend it," Lawrie huffs, through tears. "Can you. Mend it. Now."

"Not now, later," Dad says. "Open something else."

"An'. You mend it. Now."

He's really upset. I don't have to tell you, I'm enjoying myself. Lawrie's sending out these barb-shaped selfish feelings I can puff myself up with to make myself bigger, stronger. Dad's hurt feelings give me back twice the energy I put out to make myself bigger. They don't even know they're doing it. It's a real Christmas breakfast. Enjoy.

Dad says: "Shut up, Lawrie," but Lawrie shuts

up anyway, there's too many other things to open.

"COME-AN'-SEE-CANDY'S-HOUSE!" Kelly Bayley jumps up and runs in and out of her bedroom. Her mother follows her, laughing. "AN'-HER-LIFT-GOES-UP-AN'-DOWN-IT-DOES-SO-CAN-YOU-COME-AN'-SEE?"

Kelly's mother sees. In the meantime, Lawrie's batteries don't fit his Super Stunt Racetrack. Dad nips downstairs to feed the dog, so Lawrie forces in the batteries anyway, but they really don't want to go. Before Dad pounds back upstairs, Lawrie's trashed his Racetrack. The cars will never race round like they should, and no one will ever know why.

Mum reappears with Kelly. Kelly's well over the top. She loves her slippers and Art Deck, her videos and Slime Monsterz game. Most of all, she loves Candy's House, except someone went in the chimney.

"Someone went in the chimney?" Dad looks pretty crumby. He looks like he just saw a ghost.

"They really did!" Kelly covers her mouth. She can hardly speak for giggling. She makes it the funniest thing. "Someone put Poppy Pinhole down Candy's chimney," she gets out at last, "and I'm going to go and get her!"

Dad's white as a sheet since he went downstairs. He looks like a ghost himself. Now he turns to

Kelly Bayley's mother. "Helen –" he says.

"What?" she says. "Hey," she says. She looks at him. "Hey – what's up with you?"

"Something's strange – I don't know."

"What," she says, "what's strange?"

"I went downstairs to feed Nelson." He takes a breath, and I know – don't you? – what's coming. "I went downstairs to feed Nelson." Another deep breath. "And he wouldn't come into the kitchen. There's toys in the fridge, did you know? And there's kitchen knives in the wall."

Kelly reappears in the doorway with Poppy Pinhole. "Mum thinks I must've got up in the night, but I didn't," she tells Poppy Pinhole.

Kelly looks up. She's uncertain. She puts her head on one side.

"In my bedroom," she says, "why is there GRANT on the floor?"

I admit I've put them through it. I suppose you think I'm mean. I am mean of course, that's the point. I'm not really dangerous, though, I'd just like to point out. Knives in the wall is as far as it goes with me. There are other ghosts I could mention – well, I could, but I won't.

So I make it through to dinnertime with the Bayleys. Almost half a Christmas Day, it has to be some sort of record. Dinner's a real feast for me.

I know I'm in for a treat when Lawrie looks at his sprouts.

"Eat up," says Mum. "It's only three sprouts. Think of all the people who haven't got any sprouts."

"I am," says Lawrie. "Lucky ducks."

"What's that?" says Dad. "Just you think about all the people who haven't got any Christmas dinners at all."

Lawrie goes red. Then he jumps up and huffs off upstairs. I just hoover up the bruised feelings afterwards. That's what I call Christmas dinner.

Old Lawrie doesn't come downstairs again until quarter past two, by which time the pudding's well crusty. They would have to spoil everything and give him a cuddle. It's a dangerous moment, but it passes. Then they give him a choc-ice. *Silly old sprouts,* they say. *Not worth getting upset about. Not on Christmas Day.*

The afternoon's a bit so-so. A bit of aggro over telly schedules, nothing really tasty. Not that I mind after dinner. Dinner keeps me going until supper-time, no problem. By the time they're into the cold turkey sarnies at suppertime, I don't mind admitting I'm a little peckish myself. I could do with a little resentment. I'm not fussy. A tiff would do, or an argument over a present – anything, really, to see me through till the Boxing Day niggles

128

set in. I think I might be going to make it through a whole Christmas Day this time, I really do. All I need is a snack to keep me going. A scene before going to bed? That'll do nicely.

Mum looks up at the clock once or twice, but Kelly Bayley ignores her. Bum in the air, she's playing a game. No one's put her to bed until now. She's done pretty well, keeping quiet.

Mum clears her throat. "Kelly."

I'm waiting to see what'll happen. There's got to be something in this for me. It could be just what I need.

"Look at the time." Mum gets up. "Kelly, did you hear me?"

Dad says: "Come on, Kelly, time for bed."

Kelly frowns. "Can't I stay up? Please?"

"You have stayed up. It's nine o'clock. Enough excitement for one day."

"But I just want to do my Zoo Quiz one more time. Just only one more—"

"Kelly." Dad looks up.

Kelly Bayley opens her mouth. She's about to make a scene. Then she looks at me. She looks at me, and she knows.

Then you know what she does? Instead of stamping and crying and flushing up and sending out sparks I can use, she does completely the opposite. Kelly Bayley looks at me the way she

129

looked at me in her bedroom the night before Christmas. Then she goes up to Mum in her stupid panda slippers and her dumb-looking glitter wig and her brand new Christmas nightdress, and you know what she says?

She says, "Thanks for Christmas Day, Mum. It was brilliant."

"Well, it's been a funny old Christmas Day."

Too right. They only searched the house from top to bottom, Mum and Dad, and then they put away all the knives and anything else sharp you could cut with. At least it brought them together at Christmas-time. That's the way I look at it, anyway.

"Thanks for all my presents," Kelly Bayley says, "and for everything else, ever. You're my best mum and dad."

You're my best mum and dad. Can you believe that? *Thanks for Christmas Day, Mum. It was brilliant.* And old Kelly Bayley, she kisses her mother goodnight. And Mum hugs her tight, eyes closed, folding her warm in her arms. And – thanks, Kelly Bayley – I'm gone.

Families. It happens every year. Sooner or later, they get to you with some gen-u-ine love and warmth. There's no stopping them. What would a Christmas without warmth be? It'd be, well – cold. Like me.

Pretty soon now, I'll be climbing back into my freezer. Soon I'll be frozen stiff, well out of it till next year's happy shoppers come to warm me up. It doesn't usually bother me. But this year, I think it might.

Right now, the supermarket's dead. All the aisles are cold and dark and empty. The plastic strip-curtain by the deli counter clacks a bit in the draught. The checkouts loom at the far end of the store like the keys of some piano no one plays any more. I picture the once-feverish Christmas shoppers, home now with Grade A headaches and a nagging feeling that the guarantee for the joystick someone stood on went out in the bin with the wrapping paper. Christmas. Why can't it be simple?

I wouldn't mind, but they never learn. They'll do it all again, just the same, next year. The last week before Christmas they'll be back in their droves in panic mode, scrabbling for frozen turkeys in my freezer, waking me up, as usual, when shopping fever peaks. I start wondering about them all, hoping everyone got what they really deserved this Christmas. Then I pull myself up. What am I, the Christmas fairy?

I count cut-price offers for a while. Then I start thinking about Kelly Bayley. I wish I could stop, but I can't. *You needn't think you're spoiling Christmas,* she says. *It's mean,* she says, *why don't you just stop doing it?* And her brown eyes scout me up and down.

Maybe she's right. Maybe I should stop doing it. Why be a mean ghost, when I could be the Ghost of Family Feeling? The Ghost of Icky Moments? The Ghost of Going-to-Bed-Nicely?

Right now, I'm thinking maybe a change of diet next Christmas mightn't be so bad. I may just try chewing on a little goodwill-to-all, why not? Not as good as ice cream. But probably better than sour grapes, whatever they taste like. I picture Kelly Bayley snuggling down in bed, glitter wig stowed on the lamp-stand so she spots it first thing in the morning. I picture her waking up, clapping it on, rushing downstairs in her dressing-gown for Boxing Day cartoons. Hey, Kelly Bayley, you've got me thinking I've changed. No kidding. Can I come Christmas Day next year? See you in your brand-new, smartypants outfit? With your next year's novelty slippers snapping on your feet? And stick around till midnight, even, like I never did before? Would you let me, Kelly Bayley? I promise I wouldn't eat too much. I'd do anything you tell me.

So, that's about it for this year. Nothing lonelier than a supermarket at midnight on the twenty-fifth of December, so I might as well pack up right now. The freezer sighs as I open the lid. My freezer. The freezer I was looking in when I haemorrhaged.

When I was fourteen. When I was Christmas shopping. With Mum. I died on the way to hospital. But I found my way back straight away. Been hanging around ever since. The Ghost of Christmas Shopping. I tell you, it almost frightens me.

Wee Robin

Joan Aiken

This story was told to me by my Aunt Martha. When she was younger, Aunt Martha used to pay regular visits to a rich friend, the Countess of Stoke, who had been a schoolfellow of hers some years before. The Countess now lived in a big old house, Tyle Place, which her husband's family had owned for hundreds of years. The house had twelve bathrooms, my aunt used to tell me, wide-eyed, and on her visits she was always given a room with a bathroom of her own. This was luxury and splendour for Aunt Martha, who, at home, was used to share a bathroom with her five sisters.

But one year she found herself quartered in a different bedroom with a different bathroom, and her hostess said to her, "We are so sorry about this change, Martha dear, but the pipes are leaking in

134

the room that we generally give you, so we had to make the change. But still, we hope that you will be comfortable." My aunt said that she was sure she would be, the new room seemed very pleasant and the bathroom that went with it was even bigger than the one she was accustomed to.

"There is just one thing," said the Countess, "one little thing I should mention. It is best if you don't sing in the bathroom."

My aunt wondered a little what could be the reason for this, but was too polite to ask. Perhaps, she thought, the partition walls were very thin – for two bathrooms had been portioned off, long ago, from one bedroom; perhaps next door there might be quartered some other guest with highly sensitive nerves who could not abide the sound of singing; some simple reason of that sort there must certainly be. At any rate, whatever the cause, she readily promised not to raise her voice in the bathroom.

A great number of other guests were staying at Tyle Place that year, for it was the Christmas season; there were young folks and older ones, there was present-giving and play-acting, games and dancing; day followed happy day and Aunt Martha seldom sought her chamber until well past midnight, when she was too tired to do anything but jump into her bed as quickly as might be. But when she did retire she always remembered her friend's prohibition and never, when she was within her own domain, made the mistake of raising her voice in song.

But one night – near the end of her visit as it happened – the younger guests had been gaily country-dancing in the huge old raftered hall which was the most ancient part of Tyle Place. Fiddlers and pipers had been summoned from Tyle village and most of the party had been dancing until well into the small hours; then the tired players were handsomely fee'd by the Earl and Countess, they took their leave, and the young guests started upstairs to bed, some of them, at least, still wishful to remain downstairs a while longer and go on dancing. Through the closed front door they could still hear the village band gaily playing their way down the hill. The tune they played was "Gathering Peascods" which, as it happened, had been the final dance before the party came to an end. My Aunt Martha heard the music come floating through her bedroom window, which faced forward on to the approach drive.

Without thinking, Martha began to whistle – for she had a clean and tuneful whistle, like a boy or a blackbird – and, still without thinking, in her happy mood after the festivities, she plucked her nightgown off the bed, where it was laid out for her, and danced her way into the bathroom still whistling "Gathering Peascods". A joyous, lively tune.

What was her astonishment, then, to see a wee boy sitting on the bath mat by the bath, naked as a bullrush, and crying his heart out!

"Who in the wide world are you?" says my Aunt Martha.

But he cries all the harder and makes no reply.

Well, Aunt Martha could not bear to see him so cold and shivering – for it was a bitterly cold, frosty December night – so she puts round him her own woollen bedjacket and wraps him in a quilt on her bed.

"Who are you?" she says again.

But all the answer he gulps out through his sobs is: "I want my mammy! I want my daddy! I want Nurse Ellen!"

Well, Aunt Martha is puzzled at this as may be, for, to her knowledge, none of the other guests had brought a child with them to Tyle Place. But she says:

"Wait a little minute, my dearie. I'll fetch your Auntie Delia and she'll soon have ye sorted."

Then she runs along the passageway and down the stairs, to where her host and hostess are still discussing the end of the party.

"Delia, come quick!" she calls. "There's a wee boy in my room and, poor little dear, he seems clean moithered! Not a stitch on him and calling for his mammy!"

Poor Countess Delia turns white as a pillowslip.

"Oh my dear!" she says. "Just what I hoped would not happen!"

"But who is the poor child? And who are his parents? Come to him, quick, quick!"

"I'll come, my dear, but the chances are he'll not be there..."

Sure enough, when they return to Martha's room, there's no sign of the child; the jacket and quilt are there, snugged round on the bed as Martha had left them, but the wee boy is gone.

"Where can he be?" cries Aunt Martha, and runs into the bathroom. But the child is not there either and – what strikes Martha for the first time – the bath mat he had sat on is gone too; but there is still a plain blue woollen mat hanging on the warm towel rail.

"We'll never know where he has gone," says the Countess.

"But who is he? And who are his parents?"

"Dead and gone, my love, these hundred years. That's the pity of it."

"What can you mean, Delia? And who is the little lad?"

"He's Wee Robin."

So the Countess tells his story.

"He had a godmother, Lady Astoria Vane, who was the cousin of his father, the fourth earl. Lady Astoria doted on the boy. She was a great traveller, as ladies were at that time – this was early in the nineteenth century – she went to Turkey and the Lebanon, she visited Ceylon and Kashmir and many Arab lands. And from these places she used to send back lavish presents to her godson, many of which he was too small to appreciate. The line of silver elephants on the side table in the dining room, for instance, and the stuffed camel in the conservatory. And, when he was four, she sent him a magic bath mat."

"A magic bath mat!"

"Such an unsuitable gift for a four year old! Of course, nobody knew that it was enchanted. They did think, however, that it was too handsome for a child. Well, you probably saw it. It was Chinese silk, wonderfully woven and embroidered."

Now Aunt Martha remembered that she had been faintly surprised to notice that there were two bath mats, one of plain wool hanging on the warm rail, and the one on which the boy sat, glossy with colour and brilliantly embroidered.

"The fourth Earl, Robin's father, was a very talented musician. He played many different instruments, and he composed music as well. He often used to play tunes to the little boy, who, like his father, loved music. He was always humming and singing – in his bath, in his cot, when he walked out in the park. And – it is thought – one of the tunes that he hummed or sang must have activated the magic mat, which they had put in the bathroom. There was a nursery maid, Ellen Rigby – she walked into the bathroom one evening, ready to give Wee Robin his bath. There he was, sitting on the mat, humming a tune, happy as a sandhopper – and then – the next minute – there he was not! Clean vanished. They searched, of course. They called, they hunted – first the whole house, then the gardens and park, then the village. They told the police. They advertised, locally and in national newspapers. None of it was any use. They never saw Wee Robin again. Both parents died of grief. They had no other children. So the fourth Earl's cousin inherited the house and the land and the title."

"But why has he come back now? And why didn't he stay?"

"Hearing a tune sometimes fetches him back from wherever he has gone – no very happy place it seems, he always seems very forlorn and bewildered."

"Have you seen him, Delia?"

"Once, and Charles has seen him once."

"Poor, poor little creature. I do wonder where he comes from?"

"And where he goes back to? Perhaps it is a different place every time. He is still hunting for his parents. And for Nurse Ellen. There is a belief among the local people that, if you see him three times, he will stay with you. But no one has ever seen him three times."

Secretly, Aunt Martha resolved to try and see Wee Robin again. His sadness, his loneliness, his strange plight had touched her deeply. The Countess offered to change her bedroom for the last three days of her visit, but she said no to that. And every time she went into her bathroom she sang or whistled "Gathering Peascods". Once, she had a fleeting glimpse of Wee Robin, skinny and forlorn, sitting on his mat.

"Oh, won't you come with me?" pleads my Aunt Martha. "I'd look after you – I'd love you – I'd teach you and care for you and make a home for you!" But all he whimpers out is, "I want my mammy! I want my daddy! I want Nurse Ellen!"

Gone, all of them, long into the past.

And before Aunt Martha could touch or soothe or persuade him, he was gone again, back, perhaps, to where he had come from. Or to some other desolate corner of time and space.

My Aunt Martha never married. Never had a

child of her own. I think she always hoped she would see Wee Robin a third time. But her friends left Tyle Place and it was pulled down. A wind farm occupies the site. Forty great spinners stand there, whirling their arms against the sky, and if Wee Robin comes visiting there, he must find it bleak indeed.

Snowblind

James Swallow

As he waited in the chill evening air, Stefan Harmsway rocked back and forward on his heels, watching his breath make little pops of vapour as it escaped his mouth. He wriggled his toes inside the expensive socks and handmade Italian shoes that surrounded them, he clenched and unclenched his hands deep within the folds of his jacket's thermal pockets. The bite of frost that had grown with the sunset a few hours ago tickled his cheekbones along the frame of his glasses and made his face cherry-red. It was the only bare skin visible, his small countenance and dark, perfectly-cut hair peeking out of the top of a heavy, grey, tailor-made greatcoat. His eyes ranged over the small open plaza around him, the skeletal trees in ornamental planters, the vast wall of glass that was the entrance to the production plant, and the parking lot still half-full with snow-dusted vehicles. Even on Christmas Eve, his father was still working his staff, keeping them at their stations while the rest of the world was heading home.

Stefan kicked at the ground. He was unsettled and tense. It was a condition he seemed to spend most of his life in, fourteen years old and constantly on-edge, self-absorbed to the point of total disinterest in the things around him. Nothing seemed to hold his attention for long, no amusements or diversions kept him focused for more than a few days, a week or two at the most. He was constantly wary, uncomfortable in the life he found himself in for reasons he did not understand. Stefan knew something was wrong with his life; what it was escaped him.

But nothing was more alien to him than his father's work. Despite the fact that Louis Harmsway was the sole owner and CEO of GeoDyne, one of the largest biochemical engineering and research corporations on Earth, despite the fact that Daddy's company earned millions of pounds every hour, despite the fact that it paid for all of Stefan's expensive lifestyle, the boy had zero interest in it. For Stefan, the idea that there would always be money for everything that he ever wanted was like gravity; it was a force of nature, something that was as much a part of his world as breathing. He never once questioned if he was entitled to such an opulent life. It would never have occurred to Stefan that he wasn't, that something might have been wrong with his rooms full of expensive clothes and gadgets, used once and forgotten while other people struggled just to find enough money to live. The Harmsway family was very rich. That was just the way it was in Stefan's world.

And yet ... there were moments – just fleeting ones, to be sure – when something deep in Stefan's inner self rang a wrong note, warned him that things were not right, unbalanced, incorrect; but that was easy to silence when you never wanted for anything.

Behind him, Doyle cleared his throat, and the boy gave him a sideways glance over his wire-rimmed spectacles. The bearded bodyguard was a thick, stocky figure, and to Stefan he always seemed like an overstuffed doll, as if someone had taken the body of a man and then packed half as much again into it, creating sturdy arms wide as tree trunks, and a fat neck that made his bald head look like a bullet. Doyle never said very much; he was a man of actions and few words, never more than an arm's length away from Stefan whenever the boy left the family home. The big man indicated the glass doors with a tilt of his head. Louis Harmsway was crossing the reception area towards them, with a gaggle of suited men bearing briefcases, some chattering into cellphones and others offering his father sheets of paper to examine. On a trip to Rome when he was eight, Stefan's tutor had taken him to a museum of the Roman Empire and shown him statues of ancient generals, who conquered great swathes of the globe; his father looked like those men, arrogant and purposeful, striding out of the doors and across the icy plaza like a victorious centurion.

"Stefan." Louis Harmsway's voice cut through the air like a scalpel, and the boy curled his lip in reply. "Come here," his father added.

He obeyed; he always did, but the older he got, the longer he took to do it. Doyle followed discreetly behind him, like a giant shadow hovering just at the edge of his vision.

"Try to smile this time," Louis said, silencing the men around him. "It looks much better for the audience."

Stefan resisted the urge to put on a broad, lunatic grin and just nodded, watching his father. His parent studied him for a moment, as if he was fixing his demand in the boy's head with a hard stare, and turned away to look over his shoulder.

"Here they come," one of the other men said, a

hint of nervousness in his voice, "Sir, if you can remember not to discuss—"

"I know what to say!" Harmsway barked, and for a second Stefan saw his father's inner face revealed, his anger and annoyance at having to take part in this little performance.

Stefan turned to watch the approaching group of figures. GeoDyne security guards and an attractive corporate public relations expert were escorting a local news reporter and his cameraman, along with an older man who seemed very ill at ease. Beyond them, at the production plant's gates, he could glimpse the shifting shapes of a few dozen people waving banners and placards. The light snow that had been steadily falling all day seemed to glow with their torchlight, framing them in a halo.

The camera's powerful flood-lamp flicked on and suddenly Stefan and his father were in full glare of the lens. He chanced a look up and his parent put a steadying hand on his shoulder, smiling warmly. The boy felt a chill at the touch.

The reporter wasted no time. "Mr Harmsway, I'm Gareth Hicks with the BBC. How do you react to the claims by local residents that your plant is releasing toxic material into the water table?"

Louis feigned surprise. "I am shocked by these allegations. GeoDyne has the utmost respect for the environment."

"But research indicates that local wildlife has been severely affected by—"

Stefan watched his father turn the full force of his charisma on the viewers at home, with a winning smile. "Gareth, I live in this part of the world, just a few miles from here, with my son." He patted Stefan for emphasis. "How could I allow my company to pollute a place that I call home, a place where my family live?"

The older man spoke; he had the manner of a schoolteacher. "Surveys taken by the university nature watch programme have clearly shown a massive drop in animal populations since the opening of this place!" He waved at the plant building angrily. "You are responsible, sir! You're pouring poison into the rivers!"

Louis changed tack; his voice took on a hurt tone. "I would never allow something like that to happen at GeoDyne. Our corporation is working towards a better future for our children," and he squeezed Stefan again, "because they are our most precious resource." He shook his head, as if he felt sorry for the older man. "I would have been spending this Christmas evening at home with my son, but we have been forced to come here tonight to hear your comments and now my boy has to listen to these wild claims."

Stefan's father gently pushed him in the small of

the back, and with that he knew that his role in the little act for the TV cameras was over. As he stepped away he heard the older man's words ringing out.

"You play the family man, but you are only concerned with profits!"

The public relations woman guided him away from the group of people, towards a waiting limousine, with Doyle in tow. "That went perfectly," she simpered. "You really did very well there, young man!"

Stefan said nothing. This was not the first time he'd been a prop for his dad's television appearances, acting the role of the good son in the right place at the right time to make his father seem like a kindly, loving parent. In all honesty, these pre-scripted photo opportunities were among the few times they spent in each other's company; but that was just fine for Stefan. Since his mother had died, the boy had found that life alone was vastly preferable to being a part of his father's ruthless corporate world. Doyle opened the car door and he stepped inside.

"Home," he said.

They passed the knot of people and Stefan saw a brief glimpse of his father lit by the spot-lamp, his eyes hard as diamonds; then they were through the production plant's gates and on to the road. He saw the demonstrators, people whose faces had a mix of sadness, of anger and determination, their banners warning about the dangers of abusing the Earth and dumping toxins into the food chain. Even though he knew they couldn't see him through the tinted windows of the limo, they stared back at him with loathing; and in that instant Stefan felt a bolt of ice in his chest, a sudden clear understanding of them. *These people,* he realized, *they hate me because my name is Harmsway, because of the company. They hate us so much that they would sacrifice the one night of the year they should be with their family just to prove it.*

And as that cold little idea took root in Stefan's mind, a woman with grey eyes like chips of sea ice and skin pale as milk put down her placard, and walked after the limousine with steady and deliberate steps. Where her feet fell, patches of frost marked the ground like blooms of white petals.

The road was invisible beneath a patina of ice that reflected the sodium flare of the limo's headlights, and Doyle worked hard to keep the long car from fishtailing as it took the corners along the country road. In good weather, the plant was less than an hour's drive from the impressive stone mansion the Harmsway family used as their English residence, but in the grip of winter the journey was difficult. Doyle had the windscreen wipers flashing back and forth across his vision, fighting to clear the glass of the snowflakes that seemed to swarm towards it. The bodyguard grimaced and pumped the brakes as the vehicle pulled the wrong way, drifting dangerously close to an embankment as he made another turn. On a night like this, every one of these winding back roads seemed identical to each other, with what signs there were made unreadable by rimes of ice and snow. Doyle took another corner and cursed under his breath. He'd driven this route a dozen times, so how could he be lost? He changed gear and the limousine reacted poorly as ice began to build up around the tyres, and the internal heater laboured to produce warm air.

Defying possibility, temperatures as cold as the Arctic began to form around the car, as a bubble of sub-zero air enveloped it, chilling the metal framework in seconds. The bearings in the wheel hubs began to lock together as grease and oil fused into waxy clots of ice, and the engine coughed and choked. Doyle's eyes widened as fans of frost reached out across the glass windscreen, freezing out any vision of the road ahead. Something rose up in the white brilliance of the headlights, and he reflexively jerked the steering wheel aside to avoid it.

For a heartbeat, the bodyguard saw an ashen-faced woman with cold eyes; then the limousine was skidding out of control, the wheels turning beneath it, the car flipping as it hit the lip of a ditch and tumbling, coming to rest upside down in darkness.

Stefan was surprised to discover that his glasses had stayed on his head, even as the interior of the limo spun around its axis and bounced him about like a dice in a cup. He had struck his head on the door handle as the accident unfolded, and a livid bruise was blossoming on his temple, but he was otherwise unhurt. There was barely any light inside the car; only a broken lamp set into the drinks cabinet was still functioning, the contents of the case scattered over the inverted ceiling along with a broken TV monitor and other scraps of debris. Stefan could hear a thin hissing noise coming from the nearside window and he peered at it. Dark, inky water was streaming in through the seals around the door like a liquid blade.

"Doyle!" he yelled, his voice quavering. "Doyle!"

Stefan was answered by a thud from the front of the limo, from the other side of the sealed driver's compartment. Doyle had been belted into his seat when he'd lost control, and the force of the safety

152

airbag had cushioned the bodyguard from impaling himself on the steering column. Unbuckling his belt, he fell out of his seat and righted himself. "Break the glass." He coughed, spitting out a sliver of chipped tooth. "There's a hammer by the door."

Stefan looked and saw a small orange T-shaped tool in a spring-clip on the doorjamb, next to a tiny label that read "In Emergency Break Glass".

"But we're upside down, in a ditch full of water! I'll drown!"

"Do it, you little bleeder!" Doyle snapped. "I'm getting out!"

Stefan took the hammer and struck at the window, and it shattered as if had been hit by a bullet. Behind the fragments of glass came a freezing flood of brackish, oily water choked with dead weeds and clumps of ice, and in seconds it was up to the boy's neck, leeching the heat from him. With adrenalin fuelled by panic, he forced himself out of the window and out of the limo, his hands clutching at the earthen banks of the ditch to escape. Stefan rolled on to the snowy ground and spat up thick, chemical-tasting phlegm, wiping his smudged glasses on his sleeve. From the other side of the upturned vehicle, Doyle emerged, wet-through and irate. The driver swore loudly and kicked the limo; Stefan had never seen Doyle so animated before and it frightened him a little. He looked away, back at the glutinous water in the ditch, and there he saw the tip of a metal barrel, half-buried in the mud. The top of the canister was rusted and split, but the stylized GD logo of the GeoDyne Corporation was clearly visible, right above the toxic hazard warning symbol. It was then that Stefan noticed the streambed was thick with the decayed corpses of fish, and what looked like a swan, the fouled water so sickly that it wouldn't even freeze in the cold.

The boy scrambled to his feet and dashed back to the road, tripping over the skid marks the car had cut in the ice. Doyle followed him, stabbing at the buttons on a cellphone. He pressed it to his ear, then snarled and tossed it away. "Useless!"

Doyle gave Stefan a quick glance. "We'll freeze to death if we stand around here." He jabbed a finger in the direction they'd been travelling. "This way, come on."

For a second, Stefan considered arguing otherwise, but the bodyguard's expression told him quite clearly that dissent would not be tolerated. The boy hugged his dripping wet coat to himself and shuffled after Doyle. Under the cold light of the winter stars, the road ahead seemed like a tunnel into the darkness, the tops of trees meshing together and white drifts clustering around their roots. A dense fall of snowflakes filled the air with their unearthly grace, settling a blanket of deathly silence across the landscape around them.

Doyle rubbed his hands and tried very hard not to think about what he'd glimpsed in the darkness the second before the car crash. He had run the limo right into that woman standing in the road, but the instant she'd struck the bonnet, her body had vanished, like it had split into a billion particles of ice, flickering then gone. He glanced back at the road, following the tracks of the skid; no blood, no body. *I must have imagined it.*

"Wh-who's there?" the boy called out, and Doyle spun around.

"You see someone?" he snapped.

Stefan was having some difficulty speaking, his teeth chattering with the chill. "I thuh-thought I saw a person over there." He pointed. "In the tuh-trees."

"Get close to me –" Doyle began, but his words were suddenly ripped away from him by a huge gust of wind. A vast wall of cold air studded with flecks of ice and tiny bolts of hail crashed down upon them like a floodhead, and Stefan stumbled against a tree trunk. The branches rattled and cracked against each other in a thunder of snapping wood, and the dormant piles of snow were pitched into the sky. In an eye-blink, the still winter night transformed into a blizzard.

Doyle peered owlishly through the razor-edged snowstorm as a shape defined itself out of the darkness, an approaching figure. He rubbed at his face, the skin on his hands and nose turning white and waxy, flicking away tiny icicles from his facial hair. "Who's there?" he bellowed, feeling his stomach knot in fear. In most circumstances, the bodyguard was not a man given to fright. Doyle had been a soldier before he had become part of Louis Harmsway's private security force, and he'd seen action in many parts of the world, from the Philippines to the heat and dust of North Africa; but now those warm climes seemed like a dreamy fantasy, and the sight of the woman advancing towards him terrified him like nothing ever had before. It was the figure he had clipped with the limousine; her face was the colour of the snow she walked on, and her hair blew back over her shoulders like a mane of silver wire. She matched gazes with Doyle and the big man felt his heart shrink in his chest.

Stefan gasped as Doyle's hand flashed inside his coat and returned with the blocky shape of a pistol. It was illegal for bodyguards to carry weapons in this country, but it didn't surprise him to discover that his father's employees flouted that law; if what that reporter back at the plant had said, it certainly wouldn't have been the first crime GeoDyne had committed.

"Stay back!" Doyle cried, and Stefan heard a twitch of fear in the driver's voice. "I'll shoot!"

The words barely carried over the howling of the snowstorm, which hurtled around the woman in a nimbus of frigid air and ice. She walked in the eye of the polar hurricane, carrying it with her.

Doyle's frostbitten fingers were barely able to move, but the numb hand gripping the gun managed to squeeze two shots from the weapon. The bodyguard watched as the woman merely shrugged the bullets away, the hot rounds glancing off her cheek and her shoulder in puffs of ice. The wind gusted harder and then she was on him, one hand reaching out and slapping the pistol from his grip.

Stefan heard Doyle scream as the gun shattered like glass, the metal so cold that it became brittle, the raking blow catching his fingers as well. The boy was back-pedalling now as Doyle turned to run from his assailant, and so the bodyguard never saw the woman mete out her payment in kind for his attack – but Stefan did.

With an airy gesture, the silver-haired woman drew up a wide carpet of snow from the ground in front of her, which peaked and curled around itself like a rising wave of ocean surf. The icy form snapped out at Doyle's back as if it were alive, gaining on him and flooding to his ankles, rising up in coils around his legs and thighs. He turned in the grip of it, his hands coming up to shield his face, and the tonnage of snow fell down across Doyle's body with a dull crump of displaced air, crushing him under his own personal avalanche.

Then the white-skinned woman looked up at Stefan, and the boy began to run.

The storm dogged him at every step, tearing and biting at him, weighing him down with great patches of ice on his coat and his legs. A blade-sharp draught hit Stefan across the face and his glasses flew away, vanishing into the night. The boy tripped and fell, crashing forward on to a sheet of ice. He slid a few centimetres, his cheek pressed against the creaking, squealing icefield. The blizzard engulfed him, taking away what was left of his poor eyesight. His numb hands pushed against the ice, struggling to stand and failing. Stefan felt his gut tighten. Somehow, he had blundered on to a frozen lake, and now he had no idea which way to turn, which way was safety or which lead out to thinner ice.

"Boy." The voice was made out of the breaths of frozen wind. "I see you."

Stefan began to cry, the tears on his face icing

into tiny hemispheres. "What do you want?" he shouted in defiance. "Leave me alone!"

She was close; Stefan could feel her polar breath on his face as she spoke. "Your kind, boy. They disrupt the order of things in the world. You are the cause."

"Muh-muh-me?"

The white woman knelt beside him. "Each year I come south and stay a while. Then others come and take my place. This is the cycle of life. This is the nature of things."

Stefan struggled to squeeze out the words. "The. The. Wuh-winter?"

"But your kind have warped that." She growled, the ice dancing around her. "Now I am forced to stay longer and longer each year, and soon a year will come when I never leave. Understand that, boy." She touched him for the first time and Stefan's heart skipped a beat at the sensation. Her skin was colder than space. "This is the time of hibernation and rest, rebirth and renewal. But if it does not end, rebirth will never come. The world grows cold and dies, boy. Because of your kind."

She put a kiss on his forehead and Stefan went blind with whiteness. "Stem the tide, boy. Stop the poison."

"But I can't see!" he blurted.

"You've always been able to see. You just chose

not to." The voice began to fade, and with it the wind. "Your chance is coming. Use it wisely."

Stefan got to his feet and stumbled after the sound of her voice, finally falling over the bank of the lake and landing on solid ground. He shouted so hard it made his throat hurt. "I can't do anything! I can't stop the plant from dumping the waste! I'm not in charge, *he is*!"

Her last words to him were the most chilling thing of all. "We will see."

Louis Harmsway slammed the door of his Porsche and strode up the broad stairs to the entrance of the mansion. His foul temper, already close to boiling point, was not improved by the fact that someone had left the door open and he thundered inside, intent on finding a servant to fire because of it. He'd had a gutful of that reporter and the worthless tree-huggers that picketed the plant – didn't they have homes to go to? It was Christmas Eve! They couldn't even leave off their whining for just one night of the year! He shook his head. At least the boy had played his part well enough. Louis had little time for the lad – he was running a global business empire, after all – but it pleased him to see that Stefan did as he was told and appeared to have a spark of intelligence to him. He'd need it as well, because GeoDyne would be his when Louis cashed in his chips, and to have a softheaded fool in charge would be ruinous…

He reached a light switch and flicked it on, but to no avail. Harmsway cursed and ventured deeper into the building. "A power cut?" he fumed aloud. "I'll have someone's hide for this!" As he reached the reading room, he flung off his overcoat and dropped it into a chair; and suddenly he noticed the chill in the air, cold and hateful like the inside of a meat locker. Glancing around, he could see by the moonlight through the window that every surface in the room, every inch of the place was covered in a thin layer of ice.

Movement caught his eye, and even as he started to shiver, he turned to face a pale-skinned woman sitting languidly by the dead ashes of the fireplace.

She smiled, revealing a mouth of perfect teeth white as icebergs. Harmsway tried to call out, but his lips were numb and blue with the cold, his teeth chattering uncontrollably, his heart slowing as hypothermia began to take hold of him.

The woman gave him a cool stare. "Tell me," she said. "Is it cold in here, or is it just me?"

The Devil's Dozen

Celia Rees

Wolfgang Hoffman was working late in the factory of Gerhart, Bauer & Rheinstein, Dollmakers to the Imperial Court. The figure he was creating was exquisite, every detail perfect from her beribboned, bonneted head to her calf-skin slippers. Her rich silk gown rustled under his fingers and her ringletted hair shone in the lamp light like pure spun gold. She was a sleeping eye doll. As he examined her, the blue eyes blinked and looked up at him as if she were just waking. Her half parted rosy lips seemed as if they were about to speak. A delicate blush rose through her cheeks, flushing her peach complexion to a delicate pink. Wolfgang almost expected her skin to feel warm. Foolish, of course. She was made of bisque, just like all the rest. But that was his test. The ones that looked as though they were alive, they were the very best.

Once he was satisfied, he turned her over. Her leather back was stamped with the maker's mark: a high pointed crown. He dipped his pen and added his own initials, *WH*, in fine flowing italics, and under that *Lisa*. He was the finest craftsman at Gerhart, Bauer & Rheinstein, a master, and as such he could name his dolls.

His work was highly sought after, commanding far more than the average price, and that was high enough. Not that Wolfgang saw much of the money. He eased himself from his bench and blew on his fingers. His employers were as mean with their wages as they were with the heating. He flexed his hands inside the half gloves Hannie had knitted. The joints were knotting with rheumatism. It was not just the cold. Damp seeped in from the river, even though the water was frozen at this time of the year.

Wolfgang took Lisa to Frau Gerhart to be wrapped in tissue and boxed. Usually one of the girls did that, but this consignment was special. These dolls were destined for the castle. On Christmas Eve, even Gerhart and his wife stayed until the order was finished, each doll boxed and gift-wrapped for the Count's Christmas party to be held at the castle tomorrow. Children from all over the principality, all over Germany, would be there with their parents. It was quite the grandest of occasions. One of the most sought after invitations in the annual social calendar. All the children received gifts from the Count dressed up as Saint Nicklaus. The very luckiest little girls were given one of the Christmas dolls.

Wolfgang didn't care what went on up in the castle. He would enjoy his own Christmas with his beloved Hannie. They might not be rich, in fact they were very poor, but happiness did not depend on wealth and riches. They would have a wonderful time, just as good as those grand lords and ladies and their spoilt children who had everything. Better. They would want for nothing. A fat goose hung in the larder, and he had been putting a bit by every week to purchase a few luxuries. There was a rich stollen cake and marzipan sweetmeats for Hannie, a bottle of schnapps for himself, tobacco for his pipe and a Dutch cigar. Hannie would play the little mother. She had been baking cakes and biscuits and would be in charge of all the cooking. He would sit by the fire smoking his pipe, with no work to bother him.

He had been to the forest to gather a tree for Hannie and they had decorated it together with iced biscuits made by Hannie and hangings made out of bits and scraps he had brought from the workshop. Tonight he would light the candles and they would look at the white fire twinkling through the branches and think of the stars that had looked down on the Christ Child. Then they would walk though the sparkling cold to midnight service to see the miracle for themselves. Hannie loved to see the Christ Child with his Virgin Mother brought in solemn procession. She gasped in wonder as the baby was laid in his cradle to be gazed upon by shepherds carved by Wolfgang's great-great-grandfather. Wolfgang would hold her up so she could get a better look, and he would try to banish the blasphemy that had come into his mind every year since Hannie was a baby: "Never was a child more beautiful, even Christ Jesus. Never was a child loved as much, even by the Blessed Virgin Herself."

On the way back from the church Wolfgang would carry Hannie on his shoulders, for she would be tired, and when they got back to the house Hannie would hang her stocking. Wolfgang smiled at the thought of her face the next morning. In among the little wooden animals and the oranges, apples, nuts and dried fruit, comfits and sugar mice, there would be the most beautiful lady. No child in the land would receive her equal. His smile widened. She would make the dozen destined for the castle look drab and tawdry, fit only for the children of peasants.

He was lost in dreaming of how it would be.

"All finished now, Wolfgang. Let me see."

Wolfgang offered the doll for Herr Gerhart's inspection.

"She is beautiful, beautiful! Good work! Good work!"

Herr Gerhart was small and bald, chubby about the cheeks with a double chin and rings of flesh around his neck. He reminded Wolfgang of a fat old baby. He looked exactly like the novelty infant, the ugliest doll that they had ever manufactured. When he saw Herr Gerhart looking up at him, brown eyes bulging, long upper lip jutting out over his half open mouth, he couldn't help thinking that Herr Gerhart had modelled the doll upon himself.

The little man darted forward and back, clapping his hands with pleasure, beckoning his wife to admire the perfection that he would claim for Gerhart, Bauer & Rheinstein. Despite the signing on the back, it was as though he'd made each one himself. Wolfgang gave the doll to Frau Gerhart. His work was over. When all the dolls were ready, the Gerharts would take them to the castle. This personal delivery service earned them mulled wine and spice cake by the enormous fireplace, and sometimes even pleasantries with the Countess herself.

They were welcome to that. All Wolfgang wanted was to go home now. He bade his employers goodnight and headed off into the dark.

He held the doll close, tucked deep in the inside pocket of his coat. He'd been working on her for weeks, right under Herr Gerhart's pudgy little nose. There had been no time to finish her. At Christmas they worked from before dawn to long past nightfall and were hardly allowed to leave their benches, even calls of nature were strictly timed.

He crunched through the frozen streets towards the little house he shared with Hannie, but it was not her smiling face he saw as he strode through the door. His usual greeting died on his lips as his neighbour, Frau Schmidt, came towards him out of the shadows.

Something was wrong. Dreadfully wrong. He could see it in her face.

"Where have you been?" Her hands fluttered in distress, up and around her face.

He pushed past her, sweeping back the curtain that divided the sleeping area from the living quarters.

"I sent for you. I told Herr Gerhart..."

When he left that morning Hannie had been sleeping. She looked as if she were sleeping now...

He bent close, closer, closer yet, bringing his cheek right down to her lips, but he felt no hint of breath on his face.

"I came to see if she wanted anything from the

market, and found her still not stirring. She was hot, delirious, she didn't know me. I sent for the doctor, and for you..." Frau Schmidt paused, trying to recollect herself. "The doctor came directly. He said it was a brain fever. It afflicts children and it takes them quickly. So quickly." Her hands rose again like two white moths in the semi-darkness. "There was nothing he could do."

Wolfgang shook his head as if he had difficulty hearing, as if his ears were full of water. He frowned. He was having trouble understanding. Her voice seemed to be coming from impossibly far away. He could not breathe. He tore at his neckerchief, gouging his own flesh. It made no difference. He was gulping for air as if he was already slipping under water, or as if some great weight had landed on his chest. He sat down, his limbs suddenly heavy, numbness spreading to all parts of him, like some creeping paralysis.

"I'll lay her out..." the neighbour was saying.

Her movement towards his daughter brought him to his senses.

"Leave her!"

"She needs laying out. It's not fitting..."

"Leave her, I said!" He shouted again, his voice roaring up from the very depths of his being. "Leave both of us. Get out!"

She did as she was told, taking no offence at his

anger. She was a kindly soul and felt pity for him. The child, too. She'd been such a bonny little thing, as sunny as the day. To be taken so young was cruel. Frau Schmidt would be back the next day to see to both of them. She shook her head. Why the next day was Christmas! Crueller still. How unfair it was. What a terrible thing to happen, and to him as well. He loved her so much. She had never known anyone love a child like he loved that little girl.

Wolfgang sat for a while without moving, as though he were carved from wood himself. Then he stirred. He had work to do. He collected shears from his bench and returned to where his daughter lay. She looked for all the world as if she would wake and greet him yet. Her skin was still warm, but the spirit had left her. Her eyes, so bright in life, were clouding like milky blue marbles. He closed them with the span of his finger and thumb, brushing the lids to sleeping eye pose.

He cut locks from her lustrous dark hair, taking them over to his workbench, laying the coils on a velvet pad, stroking the cool soft silkiness as one might pet a mouse. Then he went to the closet. Her best dress was hanging there, pale blue silk, embroidered with flowers. The handsome gown was a hand-me-down, passed on from the daughter at the castle, but Hannie had been so pleased, so proud when she wore it. And so beautiful. No tears threatened to stain the delicate fabric as he cut into it. His sorrow was beyond weeping.

He cut and stitched and glued and wove, painting the final touches on a face so exquisite he could not bear to look at it. It was her to the life. He turned the doll over and added his initials to the stamp on the back, then he dipped his pen and wrote *Hannie* in his exact copperplate. He wrapped and packed her as if for his daughter, then he went out of the house.

The village lay in sleeping silence. His steps led him away from the darkened houses, up towards the castle standing high above the town. Its crenellated turrets seemed to float above him. They looked unreal in the cold moonlight, as if carved from sugar, glittering like the magical towers in one of the *hausmärchen* the old ladies told round the fire.

He went on through the forest. The stars gleaming through the dark sweeping pine branches reminded him of the candles on the tree he had collected for Hannie. Candles he would never light; candles she would never see. He turned his face to the black sky and howled his rage and sorrow in a cry that shivered to the stars and back again; a sound so savage and wild that the wolves in the forest answered him. Then he went on, treading his way through the snow, up to the castle.

After many rings of the deep tolling bell, a man came and opened the heavy wooden door. The footman stood, mouth half open in enquiry, face still stupid with sleep

"This is the thirteenth doll."

She made a Devil's dozen. It was done. Wolfgang thrust the package into the man's hands and walked away. The footman shouted after him, but Wolfgang went on without turning, his footsteps taking him into the forest. He was never seen again.

The next day the castle was filled with feasting, drinking, dancing and laughter. The children's party was the most joyful occasion, with jolly games and wonderful entertainments and at the end of the afternoon, each child received a gift from Saint Nicklaus. It was a time of happiness, but the celebrations were short lived. First one child then another fell victim to a sickness, the onset of which was terrifyingly swift. By the time the doctor came, it was often too late. The fever spread out from the castle, taken by the departing guests. For many years in that country, Christmas passed and no one marked it. For what is Christmas without a child?

"Very rare. Hardly ever come up, even at auction. The work of a master craftsman. One of the last he made. Highly sought after. We were so lucky to get it. Most of them are in museums. Private collectors simply will not part with them."

Theo Ryder was only half listening to the salesperson's patter. He'd already made up his mind. He was like that. His decisiveness had made the young American trader a fortune in the City before he was even thirty.

"Wrap it. I'll have it."

"The price reflects the extreme rarity..."

Theo didn't blink. It would take a chunk out of his bonus, but money was to spend, right? Besides, if what she said was true, then he was making a shrewd investment. And that's what he was good at.

"Put it on that." He handed over his platinum card. "She'll love it." He turned to the little girl at his side. "Won't she, short stuff?"

"Nice dolly."

"This doll is not for children!"

Theo grinned. He thought the salesperson was about to have a cow.

"Don't worry." He laughed. "It's not for Sophie." The little girl looked up when she heard her name. "It's for her mom. She's a collector. It's a Christmas present."

"Oh, I see." The salesperson allowed herself to breathe again.

"Yeah, it's gonna be Mommy's dolly. Eh, short thing?"

"My dolly!" Sophie's brow beetled down and her lower lip protruded.

"No, Mommy's! Hey! We talked about this. Santa's bringing you other stuff." He nudged the little girl. "Bringing you something special this year, isn't he? Tell the lady."

"Monsters."

"And?"

"Dream House for my dolls."

"No, not that."

"A bike with extra little wheels so I don't fall off."

"Not that, either. He's bringing you a little brother. Isn't he?"

The little girl didn't reply. She was suddenly more interested in the gift-wrap ribbon.

"Yeah, my wife's expecting. Anytime now." Theo turned back to the salesperson. "We know it's a boy. Had the scan. Hoping to have both of them home for Christmas, aren't we? Huh?"

His daughter didn't look up.

"Nice dolly," she said, as it disappeared into the box. "My dolly!"

Her father shook his head and grinned at the salesperson.

"Boy, can she be stubborn, just like her mother."

He bent down on one knee to talk to his daughter. "It's Mommy's doll, like I told you!"

"My dolly."

He looked down at his frowning daughter. "Not your dolly. How many times? Hey! Don't start up." The little girl's blue eyes were filling with tears, her lower lip wobbling ominously. "How about I take you to Hamley's. How good would that be?"

"Can I have something?"

"Sure you can, princess." He swung her up into his arms. 'Whatever you want.'

"Oh, Theo! She's wonderful!"

Her husband smiled, happy that his gift had pleased her so much.

"It's a something, something and whatever. I thought you might like it."

"Gerhart, Bauer & Rheinstein," his wife corrected. "I can see that."

"Her name's Hannie," her daughter supplied from over by the window. She was playing with the toys Santa had brought her. Her favourite was Baby Huggs. It was a doll really, but it looked just like a proper baby. It had rubbery skin and it cried so you knew when to feed it. You also had to change it, because it did wee-wees. For Sophie that was the very best thing.

"What's that, sweetie?"

"Her name's Hannie," the little girl repeated more clearly, in case Mommy hadn't quite heard her.

"Got a name for her already," Theo smiled. "Cute!"

His wife turned the doll over to check the stamp on the back.

"It's a Hoffman!"

"Is that good?"

"The best. I've never seen one as good as this." She peered more closely at the writing under the maker's stamp. "That's his initial right there. Should be a name, too. He was allowed to name the ones he made. Yeah. Looks like..." She took the doll to the big picture window. The leather had cracked through the lettering, making it hard to read. "Hannah? Harriet? Oh, my God, Theo!"

"What? What is it?" He came to her side, thinking that maybe she'd discovered the doll was fake.

"Her name is Hannie. Sophie's right."

The little girl beamed her satisfaction. Why didn't they ever believe her?

"How did she know?"

Theo shrugged. "The woman in the shop must have said."

He frowned, trying to recall. He hadn't been paying too much attention, but that had to be it.

What other explanation could there be? Sophie was only three; she couldn't read yet. Besides, he'd kept the doll at his office. He was just about to ask his daughter, but she was busy with her baby.

"I think he's hungry," she said. "I better give him a bottle."

"He's not the only one." Her mother laughed as the sound of crying, amplified by the baby monitor, filled the room.

"We can feed our babies together!" Sophie smiled at her mother.

"What a great idea!"

They went to the nursery hand in hand. Some of the books warned about sibling jealousy, but that didn't seem to be an issue. Sophie seemed to really love her new little brother. Now mother and daughter could care for their babies together. Buying Baby Huggs for Christmas really had been a good idea.

After the babies were fed and winded, Sophie suggested taking them out in their buggies. Santa had brought her a brand new one, with big wheels, and a swinging seat. She was desperate to try it out.

They took the elevator down to the riverside walk by the Thames.

They strolled along, nodding at other walkers, avoiding joggers and children trying out new skates and bicycles. At certain points Theo and Jenny stopped to admire the view across the water, picking out famous landmarks in the city spread out along the opposite bank. All the time, Sophie muttered and fussed over her baby, tucking in the blankets a little more firmly, talking and crooning away to him.

"Keep up, Soph, you'll be left behind!" Theo had to call her a couple of times. "You wait here," he said to his wife as they came to a bridge. "I'll go get her."

"Can I check on the little guy?" He bent down to look in the buggy and caught a glimpse of black hair. 'Who've you got in here? Oh, man!' He looked up at his daughter. "She's not for playing, Sophie. You know that! Never mind," he sighed. She looked as though she were about to cry, and he hated that. "I guess she's safe for now." He looked to his wife waiting up ahead. "We just won't tell Mom. It'll be our secret."

"Secret," Sophie echoed.

"Yeah." He checked his watch. It was time to head home. Something crunched as he stepped backwards. "What's that? Oh, Jesus!"

Beneath his boot lay the crushed remains of a hypodermic syringe. Theo looked around, picking out more discarded drug paraphernalia. His nose wrinkled. There was a downside to this up and coming waterfront location. It was getting worse than the States.

"Definitely time to turn back. Come on. Let's go get your mom."

Theo smuggled the doll into the locked glass cabinet where his wife kept her collection. He put the key in his pocket and winked at his daughter, then he sauntered into the kitchen to help prepare lunch.

They ate turkey, pulled crackers and wore silly hats. After they had eaten, Jenny went to take a nap while the baby was quiet. Theo dozed in front of the television. Sophie did not bother him. She brought out a whole pack of toys, setting them out under the glass cabinet that housed the doll collection.

"Is she ever bossy," Theo remarked when his spouse came back from her nap.

"Who is she talking to?" Jenny watched her daughter's intense concentration and bursts of animation with amused interest. She was arguing with some person neither of them could see.

"Huh?"

"Sophie."

"Search me. She's been at it all afternoon. They're all in hospital," Theo explained. A plastic stethoscope swung from his daughter's neck and she was busy bandaging a teddy's leg. "Maybe she's developed an imaginary friend. Can happen to only ones."

"She isn't an only one. Not any more."

"Baby can't talk, though, can he?"

"She hasn't done it before."

"That age there are rules?" Theo laughed. "You read too many books."

The game went on until bedtime. Then Theo transferred the ward while Jenny saw to the baby.

"All done," Theo said, as he tucked in the last sick little penguin. "OK, Doc?"

Sophie nodded solemnly from her place in the bed. One or two of the most serious cases were allowed in with her.

"Story now," she said. "Hush everyone! No talking! Daddy's going to read from our bedtime book."

Theo found his place and read until they were all sleeping soundly.

He closed the book carefully and stole from the room. All was quiet in the nursery, too. With both kids asleep, he was looking forward to reclaiming his wife for the evening. He had champagne chilling and planned to turn the lights low and play a little jazz on the stereo. It would be like Christmas used to be.

It was after midnight, no longer officially Christmas, when Theo went in to check on his daughter. In the soft nightlight glow she looked so like an angel that he felt something melt inside him. He bent over to kiss her goodnight – and recoiled in shocked surprise.

There was something in there with her. Not the usual soft-furred cuddly toy. Something hard and angular. He leaned closer and met an almost adult face looking back at him. It was that Hannie doll. She'd given him a start. His hand automatically went to his pocket. The key was still there. How could that be? Must have forgotten to lock it. Theo took the doll out of Sophie's arms as gently as he could. Jenny was still with the baby, so they might just get away with it. He took the doll back to the cabinet and this time he made sure.

Theo checked the cabinet next morning, a casual glance on his way to the kitchen, then he had to retrace his steps. She was gone. Again. He went back to the bedroom, checking his pants' pocket. The key was still there. What was going on here?

It was early. He looked over to his wife, still sleeping. The baby was quiet, but he could hear Sophie. She always woke early, but she was never any trouble, staying in her room, playing with her toys. She was talking to them now…

"Where's Mommy's doll?"

It was almost as if she were waiting for him.

"Hannie?"

"Yeah. Hannie. You were told not to touch her."

"Hannie's gone."

"What?" Theo was rocked back by Sophie's finality. "Gone? Gone where?"

Sophie didn't answer that. "She told me to do bad things."

"What kind of bad things?" Theo sat down on the end of the bed.

"She said the dolls were sick. She said I had to make them better with the spike thing. But it didn't work." She held up Baby Huggs. "Look! He's got holes all over. He wees out of everywhere."

Theo examined the baby doll. A mass of small discoloured pinpricks punctured the pale smooth latex skin on his arms, legs, even his face.

"I didn't want to do it, Daddy…" Sophie's eyes were filling, her little mouth trembling. She was building up to tell him something worse. He knew from experience.

"This spike thing," he asked, keeping his voice as gentle and quiet as he could manage. "Where is it?"

"It's under there." She groped under the bed.

"Let me." Theo held her arm.

He got down on his hands and knees. In among the picture books, lost toys and pieces of Lego lay a disposable plastic syringe. He reached for it, careful to avoid the needle, seizing the orange plastic plunger between finger and thumb. He edged backwards holding it by the barrel, keeping the thing at arm's length. It felt dirty even to touch. He dumped the contents of a plastic cup and dropped it in, wiping his hands on his tracksuit leg.

He turned back to his daughter.

"This Hannie? She tell you to do anything else?"

"She said the baby was sick..."

Theo felt his blood freeze, then he was out of there, sprinting along the corridor to the baby's room. Sophie scrambled out of bed to follow. She could tell by his face that he was mad, and that frightened her, but still she went after him. She had to make him listen so he would know what had happened.

"Daddy! Daddy!"

"Not now, honey!"

Theo was stripping the baby, checking him over, trying to do it gently so he wouldn't cry. He was awake, staring up with his solemn dark blue eyes. He looked OK, but how could you tell at that age? There were no marks, but that needle could carry anything – HIV, hepatitis, you name it. Or she

182

could have injected air into him, there could be an embolism, and what about blood poisoning? And then there was Sophie. She might have pricked herself accidentally. Theo's hands were trembling. It was all too much to even think about.

"Daddy! Daddy!" She was pulling at his tracksuit, trying to get his attention. It was all he could do to stop himself from lashing out.

He was really angry now. Sophie retreated, but he came after her, face red and frowning, hands reaching like grabbers.

"What have you done?" he roared.

"I, I did a bad thing." Her own voice was tiny, barely more than a squeak.

She cowered from him, hiding behind the padded playpen. Theo turned away, trying to control his anger. The way he felt now he could kill her, but he had to find out what she had done.

"What bad thing?" His words came out with measured menace. "To the baby? What did you do?"

"Not to the baby, stupid!" Sophie's fear ebbed a little. If that was why he was angry, then she was safe – for a while at least. "I didn't do it to him. That's what she wanted." She ventured out from her hiding place. "But I wouldn't." I said, "No, no, no, Hannie! Only doctors do that. No way!"

183

"So," Theo frowned. "So what bad thing did you do?"

"I, I," Sophie faltered, her confidence draining as the full horror came back to her. "She made me mad. Saying bad things about that – and you and Mom," she rushed on, trying to justify the terrible thing she'd done. "She said you had Georgie now, so you didn't want me. I'd had enough. So, so…" She hesitated, this was the really bad part. "I put her…

"Where? Where did you put her?"

"I put her in the chunka-chunka."

It was her name for the garbage disposal. Sophie hung her head, waiting for his anger to overwhelm her. Nothing happened. She looked up. Her father was squatting down, head in hands, shoulders shaking. Sophie went over and parted his hair to see his face.

"Don't cry, Daddy." She touched his tears with her fingers. "She was nasty. Are you mad at me? Do you think Mommy will be?"

"No, honey," Theo sniffed. He didn't know whether he was crying or laughing. "I'm not mad. Mom won't be, either. Come here." He put her on his knee and hugged her. "Compacted her good, huh?"

Sophie nodded, but she was still worried. "What about Mommy? Hannie was her present and cost lots. She'll be upset –"

"Nothing a trip to Tiffany's won't cure. Anyway," her father stood up, lifting her with him, "she's got you and the baby. What's she want with some old doll?"